AWAKENING
HIGHER
CONSCIOUSNESS

"I was very touched by the weaving together of science and myth in *Awakening Higher Consciousness*. Here are two scientists who dare to be fascinated by the power of myth and who bring us along on their voyage of discovery. An enthralling read!"

PATTY DE LLOSA, AUTHOR OF *THE PRACTICE OF PRESENCE* AND
CONTRIBUTING EDITOR FOR *PARABOLA MAGAZINE*

"A deep exploration of the psychological and spiritual meaning of ancient Near Eastern myths, with the aim of highlighting their relevance to the inner work of 'self-development.'"

JEREMY NAYDLER, AUTHOR OF
SHAMANIC WISDOM IN THE PYRAMID TEXTS,
TEMPLE OF THE COSMOS, AND *THE FUTURE OF THE ANCIENT WORLD*

"A valuable contribution to the growing body of work that overturns the still prevalent conceit that ancient mythology was the product of primitive minds."

JOHN ANTHONY WEST, AUTHOR OF *SERPENT IN THE SKY*

"Dickie and Boudreau's insights are provocative and inspiring. *Awakening Higher Consciousness* is a must read for anyone interested in myth and its meaning."

EDWARD MALKOWSKI, AUTHOR OF
ANCIENT EGYPT 39,000 BCE
AND *RETURN OF THE GOLDEN AGE*

AWAKENING
HIGHER
CONSCIOUSNESS

Guidance from
Ancient Egypt and Sumer

LLOYD M. DICKIE
AND
PAUL R. BOUDREAU

Inner Traditions
Rochester, Vermont • Toronto, Canada

Inner Traditions
One Park Street
Rochester, Vermont 05767
www.InnerTraditions.com

Text stock is SFI certified

Library of Congress Cataloging-in-Publication Data
Dickie, L. M. (Lloyd Merlin), 1926–
  Awakening higher consciousness : guidance from ancient Egypt and Sumer /
Lloyd M. Dickie and Paul R. Boudreau.
    pages cm
  Includes bibliographical references and index.
  Summary: "Explains the relevance of ancient myths to the awakening to higher
states of consciousness and enlivened experience of the world" — Provided by
publisher.
  ISBN 978-1-62055-394-7 (pbk.) — ISBN 978-1-62055-395-4 (e-book)
  1. Consciousness—Miscellanea. 2. Mythology, Egyptian. 3. Egypt—Religion. 4.
Mythology, Sumerian. 5. Sumer—Religion. 6. Mythology. 7. Religion. I. Title.
  BF1999.D4845 2015
  153—dc23
                                                                    2014038417

Printed and bound in the United States by Lake Book Manufacturing, Inc.
The text stock is SFI certified. The Sustainable Forestry Initiative® program
promotes sustainable forest management.

10 9 8 7 6 5 4 3 2 1

Text design by Priscilla Baker and layout by Debbie Glogover
This book was typeset in Garamond Premier Pro with Gill Sans MT Pro, Trajan
Pro 3, and Agenda as display fonts

To send correspondence to the authors of this book, mail a first-class letter to the
authors c/o Inner Traditions • Bear & Company, One Park Street, Rochester, VT
05767, and we will forward the communication, or contact the authors directly at
awhico@gmail.com.

CONTENTS

INTRODUCTION
THE ORIGIN
OF OUR QUESTIONS

In days of yore, in the distant days of yore,
In nights of yore, in the far-off nights of yore,
In years of yore, in the distant years of yore,
When necessary things had been brought into manifest
*   existence,*
When the necessary things had been for the first time
*   set in order,*
When bread had been tasted for the first time in the
*   shrines of the Land,*
When the ovens of the Land had been made to work,
When the heavens had been separated from earth,
When earth had been delimited from the heavens,
When the fame of mankind had been established,
When An had taken the heavens for himself,
When Enlil had taken the earth for himself,
When the netherworld had been given to Ereshkigal as
*   a gift.*[1]

So begins the Sumerian epic tale *Gilgamesh, Enkidu, and the Netherworld,* from the third millennium BCE, more than five thousand

1

years ago. These words were written in a language that we are only now beginning to understand, by people with no knowledge of, concept of, or real need for the internal combustion engine or other modern technologies. What could they have written that would be of interest, that would be of use, to us today? This book explores the ancient myths of Sumer, Egypt, Akkad, and other cultures to see how modern men and women, as we now live our lives, can benefit from ancient words.

The authors contend that these ancient myths, which form the basis of present-day Western culture and beliefs, have much to provide us in the way of knowing ourselves, or the Self, such as described by Jung,[2] Martin,[3] and Raffa.[4] The myths offer insights into who we are, who we might become, where we might strive to go, and how we might begin an effort to get there. Throughout our exploration we invite the reader to look with fresh eyes at what might seem to be familiar tales. In the end we hope that these myths will offer new life, meaning, and usefulness to each reader for his or her own explorations, internal and external.

We recognize that myths arise from astronomical, meteorological, and geological events.[5] But we present here our thoughts that the myths more importantly contain valuable information on the development of the soul within man. Questions regarding life, death, and consciousness are not well understood. The enduring question of higher consciousness may be the key to the survival of the myths, as well as to their powerful ability to create a renewed sense of the Self within our literalistic and materialistic world.

One of the key points of this book is that, for each individual, daily life involves at least two different I's. For the most part, a person wanders around without much self-awareness. At certain times, however, something becomes more active and aware within. Sometimes this results from efforts of attention, while at other times it may occur through what appears to be an accident or pure chance. This arising of awareness is a beginning, a creation, or a re-creation that in this book we refer to as an awakening of higher consciousness or an arising of

Figure I.1. Authors Lloyd Dickie and Paul Boudreau at the base of the Pyramid of Khufu (Cheops), also known as the Great Pyramid of Giza, with the Pyramid of Khafre (Kephren; middle) and the Pyramid of Menkaure (Mycerinus; smallest) in the background.

the Self. We see these moments of self-awareness as the central theme of myths throughout the ages. The ancient myths, such as those in the Bible, are not merely tales of long ago and far away. We present our case that myths refer to the intimate and immediate awakening of higher consciousness—and thus provide much-needed insight and guidance.

We follow in the footsteps of many great minds. The scope and potential of this broadened approach was set out clearly in a short book by R. A. Schwaller de Lubicz, *Du symbole et de la symbolique,* or *The Symbol and the Symbolic.* He predicts that "it is rational science, which today has reached what is already being called the surrational, that will open the way towards esotericism of a suprarational nature."[6]

This book is our personal response. It is based on our studies of the greatest of the myths, those that first appeared in Mesopotamia and Egypt and were distributed to Europeans by way of the Hebrews and the Greeks. These myths embody a quality of thought and feeling that is now being widely sought throughout the Western world. Through these studies we have come to believe that myth can provide a substantial base from which to restore a balance in general perspective to our present civilization. We have become especially aware of the need to cultivate the more sensitive and introspective sides of our natures, and to distinguish them more clearly from the external social influences that can oppose or obscure them. The frenzy, confusion, and even violence that plague our social and political atmosphere act to upset any such balance between these two aspects of human nature. In fact, it is increasingly apparent that these divisive forces threaten to destroy the delicate fabric that has been slowly developed and disseminated over long periods in the traditions that underlie our present complex society. We now recognize that myths are important vehicles in the building of civilization.

At this point we ask you, the reader, to consider your approach to this material. Will it become just one more "external" influence that demands attention? Or can you find something more profound because of it? We ask you to pause and consider whether the most important thing for each of us is the individual self, not the contents of a book or the study of a myth. We do not intend to invoke any psychological or philosophical subtlety; rather, we point out a simple fact that can make a significant difference to the point of view in any study. When I, the reader, place my attention "inside" myself, an awareness of my existence arises. Through focusing on this one deliberate act, the reader can come to appreciate that awareness of the existence of being is essential.

When successful in placing attention inside, it can be seen in the background of my attitudes, interests, and activities that there exists an observing "I" that enables a certain objectivity. This objectivity allows an inner awareness, a bridge between oneself and others. Although others seem very separate and have diverse interests that are not related to oneself, it can be seen that they must operate from this same basic awareness.

This "I" of awareness can be actively present as these paragraphs are read. This awareness can give rise to an interestingly comprehensive perception of what is being said and of the extent of agreement with it. Any paragraph, indeed the whole book, can be read without any of this awareness. The book may simply be another object of passing interest in what is a personal external world. It may also become so interesting and absorbing that all inner sense of self is lost in reading. One might even catch oneself saying, "I am not paying enough attention because I see the gradual contraction in my perceptual field to the pages at which I am gazing. While I may know that my awareness broadens as I actively strive to broaden attention, I all too often relapse into a habitual mode of reading, which is a kind of sleep. But every now and again, I can see that there exists in an inner world a sense of 'I' that is central to me, but is different and generally separate from an exterior reality—an outer world—with which I am more familiar and to which I am more accustomed."

Under ordinary circumstances it may not seem important or even relevant that I explicitly recognize this fundamental difference between my worlds. But we are now embarking on a study of ancient myths that Western culture regards as tales of wisdom. We cannot go far with such a study without realizing that much of what we encounter raises issues directly related to questions about this "I." My inner awareness may be entirely missing when I am fully occupied by the external self, which is busy with what needs to be done. In fact, the externalized side of me doesn't depend on immediate inner attention, and it seems to get along very well without the inner "I."

In these myths we are repeatedly faced with situations and individuals (both humans and gods) whose behaviors and lives demand comparison with our own. They may compel us to ask ourselves: How can I understand this tale in relation to my own life? Does the quality of my life not depend on the relation between the contradictory demands of my external, practical life, and my inner sense of self? How can this unfamiliar but logically important underpinning of my life interact with the view that has formed in me as a result of continual external demands? Can fulfilling the private part of me be balanced with the requirements of living a full life in the external world?

The myths we study in this book are vitally concerned with these questions. We have written about these myths because they warn us of the threat of refusing to study such questions in our own lives. We therefore invite you, our reader, to approach this book with a certain mode of reflection and a keen awareness of your own possible stake in what the myths may offer.

Most of us first encounter the evocative powers of myth in childhood, in fairy tales and fables. However, although myths can help us as adults understand the meaning and significance of life, this potential develops only very gradually because of distractions by both work and "entertainment." We, the authors of this book, found our lives as professional scientists virtually fully occupied, and we only gradually recognized that we needed modes of thought other than the logical and rational to pursue aspirations toward what is of most value to us, both in ourselves and in our surrounding culture. In our case, through a drive to understand the significance of some of the most remarkable discoveries of modern science, we gradually realized the necessity of broadening thought to include modes primarily encountered in myth, such as analogy. In doing so, we were amazed to find consistent themes in diverse myths addressing individual self-awareness and the awakening of higher consciousness.

The private individual awareness of an underlying "I" is only with us when our attention is turned to it. Furthermore, some memories of moments of such awareness are accompanied by a special clarity that was possibly vivid in childhood. In the light of these remembrances, it may appear that this inner observer determines whether events are remembered. The inner "I" seems to be missing when one's attention is distracted or swamped by the strong impressions of an external life. Yet an external shock may also give rise to the internal observer—indeed, may be necessary to arouse it, as myths show us. Associated events are then remembered in a quite direct, clear, and vivid way. Contemplation of this inner being may also make clear that it is always the same person who observes, as though there is for it no such thing as aging. Do space and time even exist for it? Some of the myths specifically, if subtly, engage questions about the origins of time and space and their significance for reality.

Of course, there is no question that our most "awake" moments are few and far between. Authors as far apart in space and time as Plotinus[7] and Northrop Frye[8] recognized that these moments of special clarity arise only rarely, but are well remembered. It is not easy to admit that one's ordinary self so totally forgets the sense of wonder that it experienced in moments of such seeing! Our forgetting all too easily leads us to suppose that this poorly remembered inner sense is so different from our present state that it can be of little lasting importance in our lives. It may be so fleeting that it later seems even illusory. Myths can help us appreciate the significance of these differences between awareness and being asleep.

If we tried to remain in touch with this less familiar Self, would we be distracted by our daydreams and illusions and therefore unable to respond appropriately in the external world? Or is the opposite the case? We can see that our lives are so pervaded by the apparently necessary learned mechanical reactions to external stimuli that they mostly obscure or entirely swamp our inner awareness. Is it possible to find an effective balance between the inner and outer influences? In some part, one recognizes that encounters with both are significant features of one's sense of being a complete individual in a real world. The following chapters attempt to illuminate how myths help us revisit such realizations and become more fully balanced. Perhaps the wisdom in ancient myths resides in their ability to invoke deeper impressions of the different values that exist at these various modes of awareness.

To be faithful to the myths, let us regard the inner and outer aspects of the world as two different levels, which are simultaneously available to us while we remain curiously separated from each. It is true that during most interaction with the outer world, the inner awareness of oneself, or even the "thought" of it, does not exist for us as a present reality. At such times reality exists only in overwhelming encounters with external events, and we are occupied with these challenges. The other world, the one that exists in the momentary glimpses of an inner self, is then almost an illusion. It is there only as a vague feeling of presence that, while it offers another possibility, does so only when we are somehow led to give attention to it. But while the inner world is generally only fleetingly perceived, it seems to embody a more mysterious, perhaps poetic, quality—beyond our everyday occupations but somehow consistent with a deeper sense of purpose and meaning in our lives.

This less familiar, sometimes mysterious inner state certainly has parallels with what is remembered from childhood. Both now and in memory there can be an awareness of the wish for sense and meaning that differs from the satisfaction in daily occupations. One can see the need to be more familiar with the differences between them. In fact, the inner part often appears at times of dissatisfaction, which may find expression in reactions of impatience, objection, or anger; or perhaps in daydreaming; or in mechanically following appetites; or in a wish for comfort. If one's hard-to-reach inner self disappears in the midst of daily activities, perhaps that explains why some traditions call such activities "deadly sins": they lead one to lose the connection with the inner sense of "I." In life it always seems to be one or the other, but not both at the same time. The myths ask us why this should be and whether a connection between the two levels of awareness is not desirable, or even necessary, to a sense of the whole of oneself.

Our task is to use the wisdom in myths to find a path toward cohesion and comprehension. We have chosen as centerpieces of our study three of the principal myths of the major civilizations of the Levantine regions, which contributed to the development of modern-day Western European civilization. We have available writings from the ancient Sumerians, Egyptians, and Hebrews that, thanks to developments in the art of translation in the past half century, can now be read and compared with one another with new eyes and new attitudes.

The perspective that is now possible can provide new insights into the elusive wisdom of ancient traditions. Such insights can be of use in understanding the special place of human beings in creation. In modern times, a period that the twentieth-century historian and philosopher Arnold J. Toynbee has called a "time of troubles," ancient myths can help in the search for a better sense of the meaning of life, of the Self, or of higher consciousness.[9] "Meaning" in the outside world is only an adjunct to the growing sense of need for renewed internal life. With effort we may approach an understanding of the remarkable difference between the spiritual and the merely secular—and possibly appreciate the awakening of higher consciousness within. Ancient myths contain the oldest expression of who we are. This book explores how relatively well-known myths can be re-approached as a contribution to one's internal work. The book reveals that myths can effectively support our efforts to identify and strengthen our internal sense of higher consciousness.

ONE

LIFE AND MEANING IN MYTH

Ancient myths are part of our cultural heritage. The Sumerian, Egyptian, and Hebrew myths that we investigate here have remained virtually unchanged in form over thousands of years and across wide areas of varied and changing societies. Although this is impressive, our purpose here is to determine their continued usefulness for a modern-day reader. In this chapter we explore some of the reasons for their longevity as a means of preparing the reader for the detailed discussion of the myths later in the book. Preparation is essential. We need to discover for ourselves a different approach to reading these ancient lessons.

Some of the myths that we address were originally recited to audiences by storytellers who, like the troubadours of medieval Europe, must have been gifted in their ability to convey the meaning of the tales. The prodigious feats of memory involved in recitation of the longer myths are so vast that they would surely daunt today's professional actors. To judge by the narrative forms in which we now have these myths, such recitals required many long periods of listening. It even seems likely, considering their poetic form and rhythmic repetition, that recitation usually involved audience participation in the more familiar lines. But whatever the methodology, and despite their length and intricacy, these tales drew in audiences and held their interest. People gave birth, new audiences emerged, and the stories were told again and again in an ageless cycle, even through remarkable changes in the social structure of the societies in which the stories originated. Even now the continuing popularity of the stories is unquestionable.

An active connection between the audience and the myth is an essential element in the success of the story and in its transmission to succeeding generations. Although the active link that engages the listener in storytelling may be somewhat altered when a myth becomes a part of literature to be read alone, a receptive state is also necessary when reading with purpose. When we listen to myths, are we better prepared to employ them for our own benefit in the modern world?

Some of us remember how as children we were exposed to oral readings of dramatic fairy tales or fables. We may also recall how certain tales became favorites for which audiences clamored for repetition. The warmth of the interest and the deeply satisfying emotional exchanges that arise through oral storytelling, and the effects on both the storyteller and the audience, may be an important aspect of sustaining family relationships in the over-busy modern world of computers. Oral storytelling may have played a similar role among adults in an earlier phase of the development of Western society. Yet it is clear that the particular myths that have been preserved for our study and benefit must have special characteristics that illuminate a common understanding of human aspirations. These characteristics are inherent in the content of the stories and are not dependent on their method of transmission.

In our own time, the power in storytelling that must have been exerted in ages long past might be experienced in the overwhelming sensory impacts of modern movies or in the emotional sensitivities of theater productions. Perhaps this power might even be experienced through the unconscious repetition of themes in modern television programs. The continuing social importance of enactments of life experiences in the arts is most certainly attested by the large sums of money and time spent on theatrical productions of musicals and dramas.

Amphitheaters, churches, music halls, opera houses, art galleries, and museums are major architectural features of past and present in the world's great cities, and have become focal points for tourist sightseeing. These devices are gradually being replaced for modern generations by other means of communication such as television, and the Internet. But to a large extent these modern entertainments are primarily meant as distractions, not reminders of the subtle effects and unfamiliar sensations that are intentionally evoked in myth and storytelling.

This brings us to pose a serious question: Can we realistically experience in our social lives the almost miraculous, spellbinding qualities that might have been encountered in, for example, the public hearings of the ancient myth of Gilgamesh? Although it is known to have existed in written form for at least four thousand years, the average person encountered it only in public performance. And what about the details of the origin and evolution of our world found in the creation myth of the Babylonians, known as the *Enuma Elish,* and in the more recently discovered but antecedent Sumerian versions? Most of these initially attracted the attention of nineteenth- and twentieth-century researchers who were looking for stories antecedent to the Old Testament of the Bible. Their interest was confined to primarily solving particular problems of religious lineage as opposed to understanding the power of spoken myth.

And what is so special about the Egyptian myths of creation and development? They were apparently first told in the "obscure" times before the advent of hieroglyphic writing and seem never to have been written down at all in a coherent story form in Egyptian, despite the long and copious hieroglyphic records of the society. When written down, they were represented by hieroglyphs that the Egyptians called by the word "mdw·w-ntr," or as we can now translate it, "neter's words" or "the words of the gods."[1] The stories told in these myths were very well known over the whole of the religious history of Egypt, but they were not actually presented in coherent written form until the Greek Herodotus referred to them after his fifth-century BCE visits. Plutarch presented the first coherent versions in the Greek language in the first century CE, long after the peak in Egyptian culture. From what remains in Egypt today it appears that these myths must have been incorporated in the long ritual celebrations led by the priesthood and frequently held throughout the country. Both the ceremonies and the stories they told are referred to in the many illustrations carved or painted on the walls of temples and tombs over a period of two thousand years (figure 1.1). The inscriptions and figures continued to be the major illustrations used through at least two significant social and political upheavals of the whole country, and they emerged once again as major themes of art, architecture, and literature at the very zenith of the society in the New Kingdom of the Eighteenth to the Twentieth Dynasty, circa sixteenth century–eleventh century BCE, about the time of the biblical Moses. These myths are now recognized as a substantial source of both stories and imagery used in early Greece and adopted in the succeeding Christian societies.[2] Such a succession is almost unthinkable in today's world without written texts.

Myths and storytelling must, in fact, have been essential elements in the development of societies everywhere, and must have been intentionally employed in this manner. The myths we have chosen are the survivors of many that may have actively circulated for two thousand years or more and entered into the various present-day cultures through having been recognized as important by those who felt responsible for the well-being of the age.

Manuscripts, as well as orally transmitted stories, are vulnerable to the ravages of time. Most of the stories we have chosen to review here were lost to European civilization for nearly two thousand years. They were recovered only as recently as two hundred years ago. Even the languages in which they had been written down were no longer understood. It is, therefore, remarkable that today this situation is so radically changing. Excavations of archaeological material probably began simply as adventures of exploration and treasure hunting; however, by the middle of the eighteenth century CE, artifacts from the

*Figure 1.1. The Great Hypostyle Hall of the Karnak Temple Complex,
Luxor, Egypt.*

whole of the Levantine region had stimulated the interests and efforts
of travelers, explorers, and scholars alike. A series of fortuitous accidents
led to improvements in interpreting the art, architecture, languages, and
religious practices reflected in the many writings that were exposed.

In addition, during the early years of the nineteenth century CE, beautifully detailed descriptions and illustrations of the settings and the visible remnants of ancient structures were created by Napoleon's famous coterie of scientists, artists, and scholars, who he added to his military expedition to Egypt.[3] Still, until the middle of the eighteenth century CE, the purposes for building and decorating the ancient structures of the Nile region were matters of sheer conjecture. Until then, the promise of possible access to meanings had attracted scholars and travelers to the hieroglyphic scripts on monuments and in the cuneiform records found in ancient sites from Persepolis to Cairo. (Figure 1.2 shows an example of hieroglyphs as they appear in an early pyramid.) Their interpretations led to some imaginative results.

Figure 1.2. Columns of hieroglyphs from the first chamber in the Fifth Dynasty Pyramid of Unis, showing the presentation of the Pyramid Texts in the earliest pyramids.

Following Napoleon's Egyptian expedition, it became clear that the Rosetta Stone from Egypt and the Rock of Behistun from Persia, present-day Iran, each contained trilingual inscriptions, opening the possibility of translation of the material into known languages. By the 1820s in France, the possibilities inspired the work of Champollion on the Egyptian material, and in 1846 in England, Sir Henry Rawlinson published translations of ancient Persian.[4] These advances set the scene for renewed activity in excavation, translation, and reinterpretation of much that had been neglected or misconstrued until then. The cumulative result of this upsurge in interest and activity allows us to begin to discern shadows of what was important enough to past ages to have occupied a significant part of the resources of the societies. These remarkable combined efforts now create for us the possibility of comparative study, which has a continually increasing breadth and depth, almost from year to year. We believe that this wealth of new material not only speaks of what was known in the past, but offers inspired wisdom to a world that, while open to new meanings, more often shows itself in danger of losing its sense of values.

Unearthing the Evidence and Methodology of the Initial Study

To truly grasp these ancient myths, we believe that an understanding of both their intent and their content is required, and for this we need a context wide enough to embrace our growing perception of their enduring importance. Some of the tales we study here were first written down by the middle of the third millennium BCE. That is, we are trying to determine the meaning of tales that originated five thousand years ago. This is no simple task. The tales may have passed through major social upheavals in the civilizations through which they endured, which could have brought about changes in the storylines to fit each new society's needs and expectations. We must also ask whether our Western value system is so different from that of the cultures in which the stories originated that the original intentions of these tales are obscure or indecipherable. Could our perceptions of normal have changed so much over time that important aspects of the tales have been rendered virtually unintelligible to us?

In fact, the reality of changes in the understanding and valuation of basic facts led to the publication of *Hamlet's Mill: An Essay Investigating the Origins of Human Knowledge and Its Transmission through Myth.* This volume, which assesses the differences in knowledge and understanding between modern and ancient peoples, has proven to be a major landmark in recapturing meaning from mythology. The authors, de Santillana and von Dechend, brilliantly and patiently expose the consequences that have attended the loss by modern scientists, archaeologists, and artists of an understanding of even the basic facts of the night skies, so well-known by the peoples of early civilizations. They show how our modern ignorance of these common phenomena has led to a complete misconception of the knowledge and motivation of the ancients.[5]

The authors proceed by tracing intricate details of the evolution of the story of Hamlet, so well-known to English-speaking audiences from Shakespeare's play. They follow it through a number of earlier literatures of Europe and point to the evidence that ancient civilizations, especially those that developed under the clear sky conditions of the Levant, were able, perhaps compelled, to measure the positions and times of the rising and setting of the stars and planets that occupied the night sky in relation to the movements of the daytime, life-giving sun (figure 1.3). It was in these circumstances that humans must have first perceived the seasonal path of the sun and both the night and daytime paths and forms of the mysterious moon; the more erratic patterns of the planets; and the mysterious annual movement but near stability of the distant stars—all of which are so apparently and inevitably intertwined with the mysteries of the birth, life, and death of humankind. In a remarkable tour de force, they demonstrate something of the power of the necessary common background among different peoples, accounting for the various dramatic versions of the stories that resulted.

Figure 1.3. Sun at noon sighted at the top of the Great Pyramid at Giza.

They draw particular attention to the ancient awareness of the very large-scaled and mysterious celestial phenomenon gradually becoming better known by us as the precession of the equinoxes. They lead us to appreciate the effect that these common observations had on ancient peoples, who found in the highly complex but vast and regular pattern of celestial movements the basis for the characters of the many levels of gods on whom humankind depended and with whom humans lived—exposed and vulnerable. De Santillana and von Dechend's careful study of myth reveals that the knowledge of vast heavenly movements had persisted over millennia.

De Santillana and von Dechend then demonstrate how the loss of present-day concern with all but the more dramatic events in the night and daytime sky makes it difficult for modern humans to appreciate the power of this original basis for understanding myths. Our difficulty in empathizing with the importance that ancient humans found in the influence of these inexorably changing and overriding external phenomena on problems of social and political interactions dulls our sensitivity to the remarkable insights into human interactions and perceptions that are embedded in the tales. We therefore need to question whether this ancient attribution of causes really differs from or is inferior to our current faith that social and political structures can be held responsible for events in our present-day world. Could an understanding of the more vivid apprehension by the ancients of the influences that affect us help us be more sensitive to the subtlety of cause and effect of events among our own societies, countries, people, and individuals?

The perspective afforded by *Hamlet's Mill* also helps us appreciate one of the puzzling practical problems set for us by the symbolic content of myth. Knowing that an understanding of solar and stellar cycles was common among early civilizations makes it possible to accept that tales told in quite different and separate societies could have a strong similarity of themes, even without evidence of cultural contact among them. It also explains the parallelism and persistence of myths that arose throughout the ancient near and Middle East, in Sumer, Egypt,

Babylonia, Assyria, Palestine, and Greece. Evidence of actual physical contact has only recently been confirmed in a number of cases by scattered fragments of literature found among archaeological remains.[6] Only in the past twenty-five years has it become widely known that fragments of writing found at Amarna from the reign of Amenhotep IV, commonly called Akhenaten, in the Eighteenth Dynasty of Egypt, contain snippets of the Babylonian versions of the early Sumerian story of Enkidu's descent to the underworld.[7]

Such findings add to the remarkable stories of discovery and the accounts of difficulties of acceptance of interpretation of the myth of Gilgamesh that are described in the introduction to the modern translation by Mitchell.[8] He points out how even the facts of parallelism between the ancient Sumerian and Hebrew versions of the story of the Flood were for a long time resisted in Europe, fueled by the persistent prejudice that stories told in Christianity must have originated directly from special inspiration within it. In parallel with this, we can perhaps appreciate the limitations in our present ability to accept new points of view about familiar myths; thus, the need for this chapter in preparing the reader for what is to come.

TWO

MYTHS OF CREATION AND THE AWAKENING OF HIGHER CONSCIOUSNESS

We are all familiar with creation myths of one sort or other, but we may not be all that clear on what is being created. For the most part creation myths lead the reader to a physical world of sea, stars, trees, and beings. Although we recognize that humans are interested in where the physical world comes from, it is our belief that creation myths have more to tell us about the creation of the Self within us rather than the world of water and rocks. In this chapter we provide necessary background to myths and continue to prepare the reader to look at well-known myths in a new way that will focus more on the higher consciousness within us.

We begin here an examination of the earliest written myths: those that appeared in ancient Sumer and Egypt. The oldest literary versions of the Sumerian myths were written on cuneiform tablets in approximately 2500 BCE, although shorter stories and poems are known from the fourth millennium BCE—that is, six thousand years ago. Egyptians developed a parallel writing system at around the same time, in the predynastic period. Egyptian creation myths are better known because of the more extensive excavations and research in the region. In both cases there are problems with missing fragments of the writings, intentional and unintentional alterations by scribes, as well as potential faults in interpretation by translators. See appendix 1 for a more detailed treatment of the lineage of their myths. Nevertheless, when viewed together the writings of these two ancient cultures supply us with a useful perspective for exploring the impulses that led to myth creation as they relate to the awakening of higher consciousness.

The Origin and Evolution of the Sumerian Creation Myths

The *Enuma Elish* is the title given to the Babylonian myth of world creation and organization that is based on earlier Sumerian myths. The few available Sumerian creation myths usually appear as fragments inserted into the beginnings of other important Sumerian tales. They are very sparse in their details. In an effort to broaden our understanding of the Sumerian fragments, we also look here at the derivative myths from the distinct subsequent Akkadian culture. This very different culture replaced the Sumerian one approximately one thousand years later, during the time of the founder of Akkad, Sargon the Great, 2334–2279 BCE. The myths were passed on to Babylonian literatures from the time of Hammurabi, circa 1750 BCE.

Sumerian words were written in cuneiform glyphs. Figure 2.1 shows a small Sumerian tablet from the British Museum with recognizable glyphs. These glyphs convey complex ideas at various levels of meaning (see appendix 2). Modern scholars did not learn of the Sumerian culture until the middle of the nineteenth century. Kramer's groundbreaking work exposed the world to a very sophisticated culture with highly organized institutions, one capable of embracing and expressing high moral values and thoughts.[1] Yet, more recent translations provided by the online Electronic Text Corpus of Sumerian Literature (ETCSL) show how far we have come from the early concepts.[2] In the hands of the earliest Christian translators, Sumerian writing was often turned into a rubbish of confused thoughts, making

Figure 2.1. Sumerian tablet. The first word of the text is An.
British Museum.

it a challenge to probe the real intent of these precious snippets from the earliest written words.

For example, the earliest translations of Sumerian pay little attention to distinctions between the netherworld and the underworld, or to how each is related to the earth. We must look at the cuneiform

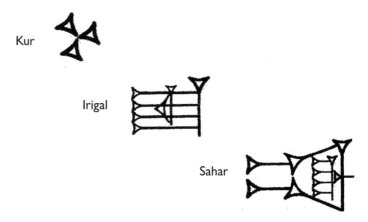

*Figure 2.2. Sumerian cuneiform glyphs
for the words* kur, irigal, *and* sahar.

originals to establish the meanings. The three glyphs *kur, irigal,* and
sahar (see figure 2.2) all have meanings related to "land," "earth," and
"soil," but the first two are sometimes translated as "underworld,"
sometimes as "netherworld." *Kur* frequently indicates "underworld" or
"underground," but it may also signify an unnamed region beyond the
world of perception, the Sumerian netherworld similar to the Egyptian
Duat. *Irigal* is additionally quoted as referring to both the "grave" and
the "great city," two concepts that we do not equate in English. We
briefly note such problems here as a warning of the pitfalls of using
unsupported translations.

To better explore the importance of such Sumerian concepts in
creation myths, we use the original Sumerian translations by Kramer
as well as four other sources.[3] Our most recent source has been the
ETCSL, which gives short original names and transliterations along
with translations (figure 2.3).[4] A third source, *The Babylonian
Genesis,* written by Alexander Heidel, became well known in the mid-
twentieth century CE because it included comparisons of the translations with biblical texts.[5] Heidel intended his work for nonspecialists,
hoping to make clear the heritage of some of the well-known Hebrew

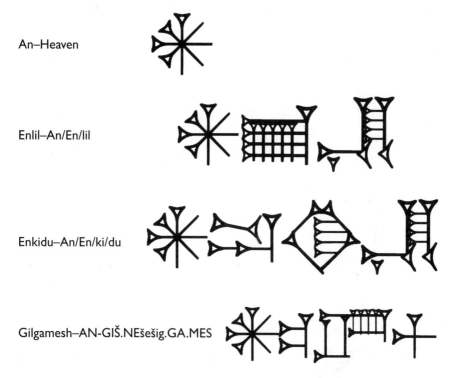

An–Heaven

Enlil–An/En/lil

Enkidu–An/En/ki/du

Gilgamesh–AN-GIŠ.NEšešig.GA.MES

*Figure 2.3. Sumerian names in cuneiform glyphs.
Images from the Electronic Text Corpus of Sumerian Literature.**

stories. Our fourth source is a version published by Jacobsen, who, with wider vision, sees myths as both stories and vehicles of religious belief.[6] Myths have expressed and influenced religious beliefs and must once have been the primary means of communicating them. For insight into the earlier Sumerian myths, Jacobsen uses supplementary information in the hymns and related poetry of the third and second millennia BCE and in scattered bits of traditional stories from as early as the fourth millennium BCE. Myths also served the wider purpose of general education and entertainment throughout the Middle East and in this sense may provide the most information for modern interpreters. Because of Dalley's sensitivity to this view, we used her recent

*See http://etcsl.orinst.ox.ac.uk (accessed January 12, 2015).

Figure 2.4. A magnified image of a pressing from a cylinder seal from the Sargonid (Akkadian) period, third millennium BCE, commemorating the return to fertility in the new year. The sun god Shamash, who can be seen arising out of the mound in the center, is greeted by Inanna as a vegetation goddess, her shoulders sprouting rays of vegetation. On the plain is a hunter with his lion. To the right is the god Enki (the Akkadian god Ea) with a Janus-headed attendant; he restrains the storm bird Zu, the adversary who stole the Tablets of Destiny; the animal at his feet is a ram (note the horn). British Museum.

translations as a fifth source.[7] She offers alternative translations and significant commentary on a number of the passages.

In addition to the written text, pictorial representations of the material are available. The Sumerian culture produced a large number of *cylinder seals,* small baked clay artifacts that contain intricate embossed images that could be rolled onto soft clay to leave an imprint. By the end of the third millennium BCE, toward the end of the Sumerian society as a political entity, cylinder seals were in common use. Seals mostly identified ownership of commercial goods, but the intricate and delicate carvings of gods on the later seals suggest that these careful representations were of value in their own right.[8] See figure 2.4.

Taken together, all of this material provides us with a sufficiently detailed account of the original Sumerian myths to better appreciate the range of impulses, methods, and objectives that myths reflect.

The Beginning in Sumerian Creation Myths

Sumerian creation stories envision the process of creation as taking place in a formless chaos, sometimes called a void. They describe it as limitless, undifferentiated waters. There is no creation of a "something" from "nothing" that gives rise to materiality, as is implied in the modern big bang theory. Although the Sumerian myths seem at first to sidestep certain questions and provide only partial explanations, it is clear that parts of the tales are missing from our sources and probably were not written down.

Some of the detail omitted in the Sumerian texts is referred to in other documents and artifacts from the later third millennium BCE. For example, here is a short account inserted into the introduction to the early Sumerian epic tale, *Gilgamesh, Enkidu, and the Netherworld*, as translated in the ETCSL:

> *In days of yore, in the distant days of yore,*
> *In nights of yore, in the far-off nights of yore,*
> *In years of yore, in the distant years of yore,*
> *When necessary things had been brought into manifest*
>   *existence,*
> *When the necessary things had been for the first time*
>   *set in order,*
> *When bread had been tasted for the first time in the*
>   *shrines of the Land,*
> *When the ovens of the Land had been made to work,*
> *When the heavens had been separated from earth,*
> *When earth had been delimited from the heavens,*
> *When the fame of mankind had been established,*
> *When An had taken the heavens for himself,*
> *When Enlil had taken the earth for himself,*
> *When the netherworld had been given to Ereshkigal as*
>   *a gift;*

When he set sail, when he set sail,
When the father set sail for the netherworld
When Enki set sail for the netherworld
Against the king a storm of small hailstones arose,
Against Enki a storm of larger hailstones arose.
The small ones were like light hammers,
The large ones were like stones from catapults (?).
The keel of Enki's little boat was trembling as if it were
*   being butted by turtles,*
The waves at the bow rose to devour the king like
*   wolves,*
And the waves at the stern were attacking Enki like a
*   lion . . .*[9]

In this myth we find the separation of land and water, which symbolizes the first steps of creation. This is captured in the image of the mound arising out of the undifferentiated waters (figure 2.4). We find this image later in the Egyptian and Christian myths. After this brief rhythmic but dramatic introductory passage, alluding to details of creation and possibly to two or three other, previously known stories, the text states that it will tell of further events.

Note that in this fragment alone we have mention of the basic division of the world into three levels: the heavens, the earth, and the netherworld. This world in its entirety is, of course, surrounded by what remains of the undifferentiated waters. The brief text also mentions four of the important gods: An, Enlil, Enki, and Ereshkigal. The first three are of those select few that, according to the Sumerians, "determine the fates" of the living gods and later humans, while the fourth, Ereshkigal, becomes queen of the netherworld, kur, which humans may enter upon death, and which is also a place entered by the gods under certain conditions.

Enki's parentage is less certain than that assigned to his "brother," Enlil—possibly they had different mothers but the same father, An. It is even possible that such vagueness is explained by Enki's actual arising having taken place at a very early stage in Sumerian myth development, and only later was he taken into the main panoply as one of the four major deities, along with Enlil, An, and Ki (Ninhursag), to "determine the fates."

In the available collection of Sumerian stories, Enki is contrasted with his "brother," Enlil, who, as god of air, was also a god of tempests and storms. Enlil was an exceptionally powerful god who eventually was considered superior in power to his predecessors, including the first of all the Sumerian gods, his father, An. In contrast with Enki, however, he was unpredictable and erratic, demonstrating forthright actions that could become violent. In one story he was held responsible for deliberately permitting the Flood that nearly destroyed humankind. In this case, Enki, who did not act in a direct or violent manner, used his power of "the word" to bring about a desired result: that is, he saved humankind and earth-dependent animals from the Flood by speaking in a dream to Ziusudra, one of the representatives of humankind for whose creation Enki had been partly responsible.* He alerted Ziusudra to the incipient devastation and proposed in the dream the building of the "ark." Ziusudra was thus responsible for the protection of all living creatures, and his ability to "hear" Enki is an important element of the story. After the Flood Ziusudra and his wife became unique examples of humankind, and Enlil granted them immortality.

There is no explicit reference to further details of the created world either in the myth to which this is an introduction or in any other Sumerian myths known to us. Other myths do make general introductory allusions to the same creation theme, but there is nothing more actually told about it. This repetition of themes from earlier myths must surely have been quite intentional, to enable hearers, who ordinarily had no libraries or books, to recognize that the story they were about

---

*Dalley, in *Myths from Mesopotamia*, says that Ziusudra is the name of a Sumerian king called Utnapishtim in the later Akkadian literature and Atrahasis in the still later Babylonian.

to hear fit within the context of other tales, perhaps ones told at other celebrations. Because the detailed stories we are looking for are missing from the existing Sumerian texts, later in this chapter we use the derivative *Babylonian Genesis* of Heidel[10] and various stories translated by Jacobsen[11] and Dalley.[12]

In the Babylonian texts, the gods that represent the arising of consciousness in the waters are named Apsu (the Sumerian An) and Tiamat (the Sumerian Ki, Mother of Creation). These two are, respectively, the father and mother of all the gods, although the fact that Tiamat does not appear in the above-quoted introduction to the Sumerian myth alerts us to the fact that the Babylonian story is different.

In the Babylonian accounts, it is said that Apsu represents "the sweet waters" of the terrestrial abyss (the Sumerian *abzu*); Tiamat is the separate "salty waters" of the ocean. These two forms of water come together at the mouths of the Tigris and Euphrates Rivers. Especially near the mouth of the more turbulent and silt-laden Tigris there must have been ample visual evidence of active, even vigorous, eddying and mixing between salt and fresh water. This Babylonian image of the first creation resulting from the mixing of the two waters is particularly turbulent. A sense of power underlies this interaction of two opposites in the process of creation.

The Babylonian authors may have been especially aware of the violence in the beginnings of society. Turbulence among positions of power had been experienced throughout Mesopotamia during the conquest of the whole of Assyria, Sumer, and parts of Elam, first by the Akkadians and then by the Babylonians, which brought to an end the previous struggles among city-states in Sumer. The image of turbulent waters may have been viewed as a justification for the unprecedented upheaval that characterized the transition from Sumerian to Babylonian society.

In a later version of the creation story presented by Heidel, creation of the first two beings is followed by the creation of a third being, called Mummu, who, Heidel suggests, might be their son.[13] In Dalley's translation:

When skies above were not yet named
Nor earth below pronounced by name,
Apsu, the first one, their begetter
And maker Tiamat, she who bore them all,
Had mixed their waters together,
But had not formed pastures, nor discovered reed-beds.
When yet no gods were manifest,
Nor names pronounced, nor destinies decreed,
Then gods were born within them.[14]

This is all we have that tells of the first part of the act of creation in the Babylonian epic of creation. Unlike the Sumerian version, the Babylonian tale elaborates many more details of a creation sequence, which we will consider below, including a god, Marduk, unique to that society.

The Egyptian Creation Equivalents

Creation myths from ancient Egypt have a long history. There are strong allusions to them in the earliest writings that appear on the walls of the chambers in the Pyramid of Unis, last pharaoh of the Fifth Dynasty.[15] See figure 2.5 for an example of the early hieroglyphs. This collection of verses is called the Pyramid Texts and appears on the walls of other Old Kingdom pyramids. The later Middle Kingdom Egyptians copied and developed the texts with little change and inscribed them onto temple and tomb walls, parchments, and mummy wrappings. Over time the texts were embellished with some slight additions and with extensive figurations used on wall paintings and inscriptions. These myths are recognizable in the Eighteenth and later dynasties of the New Kingdom. The content of these Old Kingdom Pyramid Texts has thus found its way into the extensive literatures of the civilization and can be seen as the basis for certain Coffin Texts of the Middle Kingdom and for much of the Book of Coming Forth

Figure 2.5. A close-up view of the wall of the tomb of Unis.

by Day, known to have existed in the earliest times of the society but reappearing in a major recension with "commentaries" in the New Kingdom in the Eighteenth Dynasty.

While the Pyramid Text and the early temple art led to elaboration of the story of creation in the customary exoteric mode of storytelling, it also provides us more clearly with particular examples of how myths were, from their beginnings, intended to represent our individual coming-to-a-consciousness of ourselves from a "pre-creation" form of inattentiveness or sleep. That is, from a purely exoteric standpoint, the idea of creation consists of a symbolic description of the origins of living humans or gods, and indeed, the question of "origins" is a natural focus of interest for all of humankind.

Creation stories may also prompt us to inquire into the experience of awakening from the sleep of inattention that prevails in so much of our ordinary inner life. This inattentive state contrasts sharply with the sometimes vivid awareness of a living consciousness of ourselves.[16]

In addition to texts seemingly devoted to origins, creation, and arising, it seems that in Egypt, mystical passages that cannot be sharply differentiated from creation myths are also found in texts once thought to be addressed to the recently dead pharaoh, perhaps for use in connection with his funeral rites. It is important to remember that the Egyptian view of life was specifically directed toward "the spiritual." Thus, the text that for more than one hundred years has been mistitled the Book of the Dead by archaeologists, because they thought it was intended to support and guide the newly dead in whose tomb it appeared, has been more accurately referred to by the title Book of Coming Forth by Day.[17] We now realize that there are no signs of any of the pharaohs being interred within the pyramids. Burial of mummified remains was confined to structures built specifically as tombs, which raises new questions about the purpose of the Pyramid Texts.

It has been evident for many years that the pharaohs were deeply involved in the preparation of both pyramids and tombs throughout life. Now modern scholarship, in the continual process of reinterpreting the Pyramid Texts, recognizes that they include much that was addressed to special conceptions of both life and transformation of the soul and spirit that is called *akhification*. In fact, many texts use the phrase "You have not gone away dead, you have gone away alive."[18]

Given these findings, there is now new understanding that the Book of Coming Forth by Day was based on texts that hailed the pharaoh as though he were more fully alive than ever before. It appears that at least some of the Pyramid Texts may have been addressed to the pharaohs as carefully "prepared" individuals before their "deaths." That is, in these texts the priesthood taught the pharaoh to recognize various levels in his living consciousness. Some of these levels are of an esoteric nature, understandable only by others who have undertaken a similar process. We refer to these levels collectively by the single word *spiritual*. It thus appears that the process of education for pharaohs, which later included other important officials, addressed what the Egyptians regarded as an essential passage of the soul into the mysterious world of the Duat (netherworld), which leads to its "rebirth." This was also seen as a form of "creation." Creation and rebirth are one and the same. We continue to be interested in uncovering the esoteric meanings for these myths and rituals, which have the capacity to awaken the interests of audiences of all times and address modern questions. We deal more extensively with tales involving the Duat in chapter 7.

Exoteric and esoteric modes of comprehension are both important in our attempts to delve more deeply into the role of myth in our cultural, social, and psychological development. That is, both play roles in developing both indirect and direct knowledge. The exoteric motive is familiar to us as indirect knowledge. The esoteric point of view is less familiar in our time, but once aspects of it that affect an "awake" as opposed to a "sleeping" living state have been recognized, this mode can also be seen as ubiquitous. Their use in funeral texts does not come as any particular surprise to the modern mind, although an understanding of just what is intended by the elaborate Pyramid Texts directions has been a much more difficult question to answer satisfactorily. In the Western world both exoteric and esoteric points of view can also be detected in the creation myths of the Hebrews, which we address in chapter 3. The Babylonian, Egyptian, and Hebrew myths were clearly intermingled by the New Kingdom of the Eighteenth to Twenty-second Dynasties, circa 1550–1050 BCE.[19]

Several versions of creation stories arose in Egypt in the different temple centers that flourished during the third and second millennia BCE, each with its own chief deity: Memphis (Ptah), Elephantine (Khnum), Hermopolis Magna (Thoth), and Heliopolis (Atum). All, however, see the "beginning" in the same way as it was seen in Sumer. That is, creation begins in the midst of the void, again represented as primeval endless waters. The Egyptians called these waters Nun (figure 2.6). We will first discuss the creation stories centered in Heliopolis.

Figure 2.6. Detail of Egyptian mound scene showing the hours of the night, from the tomb of Ramses I. Note the wavy lines indicating water. Compare with the Sumerian motif in figure 2.4.

The Heliopolitan Version of the Egyptian Creation Myth

The textual references we use here are found in the Book of Coming Forth by Day. This collection of Egyptian writings is as much a paean of praise to the *neters** and to eternity, as it is a funereal text.

Two references are of immediate importance, one in chapter, or Utterance, 85, the other in chapter 17. In chapter 85 we read:

> *I am Ra who came forth from Nun,*
> *The divine soul who created his [own] members. . . .*
> *I created myself in Nun in this my name of Kephrer,*
> *I came into being in it in the form of Ra.*
> *I am the Lord of Light.*[20]

---

*The early translators translated the Egyptian letters "ntr" into the more familiar word *gods*. Throughout this book we stick to the translation "neter" for direct quotes from other authors. We also use the word *god* when referring to the higher deities of Ra, Atum, Osiris, and Horus. We use the words *god* and *gods* when referring to deities of the Egyptians and from other traditions. For all other references to Egyptian deities we use the word *neter*.

In chapter 17, often regarded as the most esoteric of the chapters, we read:

> *I am Tmu [Atum],*
> *In rising up. I am the only One,*
> *I came into existence [kephrer-nue] in Nu.*
> *I am Ra in his rising up in the beginning . . .*
> *in rising up, the pillars of Shu had not yet come into*
>   *existence.*
> *he was upon the height [mound] of him who is in*
>   *Khemennu [Hermopolis].*
> *I am the Great God who created himself*
> *In this Nun, he created his name, "Father of the gods"*
>   *as god.*[21]

First to note here is the reference to "mound." We draw the comparison of this word to what we have previously seen in the Sumerian myth about the first steps of creation. The use of this image in these two great cultures highlights its importance and is reflected in the later occurrence of the separation of the earth and the heavens in the Christian Genesis story.

Here we find the principle of creation given both the name Ra, the Egyptian word for sun, in chapter 85, and Atum, or Tmu, in chapter 17, which, according to Rundle Clark, means "the Complete One."[22] Note the subtlety involved: only through the act of "becoming," as the neter Kephrer, does completion become manifest in various ways. In chapter 85 we discover that one of his becomings is as the Lord of Light, who is also named Ra, the god of the sun. Such references place this description firmly in the tradition of the major temple in Heliopolis. Yet the reference in chapter 17 to the "mound in Hermopolis" also places this god in the tradition of the temple in Hermopolis, where the major deity was Djeuti (Thoth), associated with the moon. That is, we have two versions of creation referred to in separate parts of the Book of Coming

Forth by Day, evidence that there was no one "standard" Egyptian creation myth, but several myths embodying various aspects of the creative act. We reserve further reference to the similar, but alternative, Hermopolitan version for the next section.

Here we note that Atum is named as the primordial "One," and in other parts of chapter 17, repeated references to the "uniqueness" and "aloneness" of his place confirm this. In other instances his name even seems to be applied to the original "mound." But in considering this concept of the original "One," he is also named as the neter Kephrer, the "Becoming One," frequently shown on wall paintings as well as in hieroglyphic writing in the form of a scarab beetle. The scarab was a symbol of creation, based on the observation of their use of dung balls in their reproductive cycle, which captures the functionality of creation from the undifferentiated. Thus, the idea of creation arises in Nun, becomes distinguishable from the void, and manifests as the unique, living "One," Atum. The texts indicate that Atum is, in fact, three beings simultaneously: the manifest "One," a being with the impulse to become a separate individual and a representative of light. Light is usually considered to be a reference to the sun, but the mention of Hermopolis appears to refer to the moon as well. In any case, it is made clear that the original impulse toward creation is named Atum-Kephrer-Ra, a "three-in-one" entity.

According to ancient numerology, such a threeness is not manifested in our material world. In the beginning world, this threefold entity, conceived by the Egyptians as a trinity, has the potential for creation but is not yet separated from Nun, the void in which it appeared. In fact, in some cases Naydler suggests that this "One" should be regarded as four in one, with the name Nun added to the other three (see also appendix 3).[23] When we apply this dynamic to the concept of self-awareness, one can see the flowing together of the elements that have been vivified and expressed in the initial act of arising of the Self or awakening of higher consciousness. The principle of creation has placed itself in a position to support its essential expression that is "genesis."

While the notion that numbers represent qualities may not seem logical to our modern minds, it is an ancient idea. To follow this kind of thinking, it is necessary to distinguish between our ordinary use of numbers for counting and the concept that numbers represent qualities. The numbers used in the Egyptian creation myths express aspects of the process of creation. The idea of three-in-one is found in many theologies and is still well known, although perhaps not well understood, in the Western world. In Christianity it is found in the Trinity of Father, Son, and Holy Ghost.[24] While retaining its traditional meaning, the trinity requires an observer, which results in the recognition of it as a quaternity. At this point, it is enough to know that the qualities of number must be subjected to further transformations before it can manifest in the world of solid, three-dimensional objects, our material reality. For a more detailed examination of number systems, see appendix 3.

Keeping the subtleties of Egyptian numbers firmly in mind, we may view the trinity of Atum-Kephrer-Ra as a new unity leading toward further creation, not only of the world of the neters, but eventually also of humankind. The Pyramid Texts take up the subject, recognizing that Atum, as the beginning "One," or unique god, gives birth to the first pair of children, Shu and Tefnut, respectively male and female, through two acts. One is an act of masturbation, the other, expectoration. In the first quotation below emphasis is on the fact of Atum's androgyny and on the "pleasure of emission":

> Atum was creative in that he proceeded to masturbate
>   with himself in Heliopolis;
> He put his penis in his hand that he might obtain the
>   pleasure of emission thereby,
> And there were born brother and sister—that is Shu
>   and Tefnut.[25]

In the second quotation, this same Atum gives birth to, cares for, and shelters the first beings:

You spat forth Shu, you expectorated as Tefnut,
You put your arms around them in the act of
     Ka-giving,
So that your Ka might be in them.[26]

Rundle Clark points out that in this way the Egyptians recognized how the reproductive aspect of Atum's creation was underlain by the mystery of life itself, reflected in the Breath of the Divine Soul.[27] Thus masturbation and expectoration are used together to describe how this first "One" shows in itself the capacity to generate two. The resulting production of the male-female pair is the first recognition of the duality or polarity that is inherent in the multiplicity that is to follow.

In the Pyramid Texts, the neter Shu is the most important new creation and represents an arising of the properties of "air" and "space" in the universe. Not, of course, space as we know it, because the world had not yet been created. Rather Shu may be some form of "bubble" in which "air" appears for the first time, an abstract notion of space that is not related to the infinite Nun, a place of unspecified origins. Shu is also representative of the "breath" accompanying the arising of the divine in the "life" that is now clearly present and separated from the original "One" of the universe. The Pyramid Texts engraved or embossed on the stone walls of Old Kingdom pyramids (see figure 1.2 on page 15) were developed hundreds of years later into what is known as the Coffin Texts written on papyrus. Shu is more explicitly seen as "the Eternal One"—life itself, and the mediator between the original "One" and the multiplicity of subsequent created creatures. Shu's twin, Tefnut, appears in the Pyramid Texts principally as the mate of Shu; she seems to represent moisture in the form of a moist vulva. In the later Coffin Texts she becomes Maat, a neter equally as important as Shu, representing the principles of cosmic order, love, and justice, especially revered in any idea of creation throughout the entire Egyptian civilization.[28]

The next act in the process of creation consists of the birth of Nut and Geb, children of Shu and Tefnut. Nut becomes the heavens, or the sky, and her mate and consort, Geb, is the earth. Initially they were said to have been born as a conjugal pair, a theme that Rundle Clark notes is also frequently employed in Mesopotamian myths. Shu, while representing air, brings the idea of air and space into actuality by the act of separating the newborns, air becoming the space created between the heavens and the earth.

This act of separation, while clearly important for the biological generation of living conditions, is also significant for another reason that is rarely recognized. That is, this act of separating Atum's grandchildren also introduces the "pain" of separation into the world. In the interests of further creation, Shu, by separating the two lovers, in spite of their constant longing for a return to eternal union, demonstrates that in the lower world, and presumably the part of it in which humankind eventually lives, pain is an unexpected consequence of the "incompleteness" that is an inevitable aspect of separation. That is, the two aspects of the story of creation show that world order is maintained by balancing the pleasure of Atum in the production of Shu and Tefnut against the pain caused by Shu's separation of Nut and Geb. The creation of our world of manifestation, made necessary by the requirement for a space in which life can be supported, is coeval with the arising of pain.

In the creation sequence this separation event is followed by the birth of the four neters responsible for the principles that guide the interactions of humankind. Osiris (figure 2.7), Isis, Seth (figure 2.8), and Nephthys are born as a consequence of the separation of their parents, Nut and Geb. These four neters are the final ones, created in the texts emanating from the Heliopolitan temple center. Because we will be studying them and their position in relation to the world of humankind in chapter 5, we leave any further elaboration of the Egyptian Heliopolitan creation events at this point. We simply note that in this portrayal of the neters, ideas of opposites—separation with reconciliation, satisfaction with pain and suffering, love with jealousy, and many more dichotomies—find their full expression and imply the need for reconciliation.

Figure 2.7. Osiris.
Illustration by Jeff Dahl.

Figure 2.8. Seth. Detail from the Karnak
Temple Complex, Luxor, Egypt.

Non-Heliopolitan Egyptian Creation Motifs

Early commentators on the Egyptian myths originally assumed that different myths appearing in the different coexisting centers would show a natural competition between temples for the loyalty and support of adherents to particular beliefs. But this expectation was not supported by further collections, and the idea seems to have virtually disappeared during the twentieth century, perhaps because improvements in translation have allowed a subtlety of parallel interpretations that eventually was appreciated by most of the authors we have identified. Contributions of Frankfort,[29] Rundle Clark,[30] and Naydler,[31] in particular, have all indicated clear relations among the myths of the various centers. Interpretations illustrate a perceptible, orderly, and long-term cooperative development of the Egyptian civilization, one that is reflected in the uses made of its chief symbols and myths, and one we need to learn to appreciate.

Differences in the presentation of various neters and events in the stories of creation represent a fuller representation of the complexities in spiritual and psychological affairs. A realistic appreciation of this complexity requires many different points of view to be developed, assimilated, and understood together. These different centers of teaching must have maintained a sufficiently close contact to support comparisons among the variations in the forms and images used, particularly in religious celebrations. Such variations undoubtedly led to a more comprehensive understanding of the phenomena being described.

So far, we have depended on the presentations of the Heliopolitan temple center to provide us with reference points for a study of myths of creation and their developmental changes. This is at least partly because teachings related to them are available in the extensive Pyramid Texts and are supplemented by many beautiful wall illustrations and decorated sarcophagi and mummy wrappings. It is natural to expect that the content and style of stories would have evolved over the long time periods involved in the history of Egypt. Yet a careful study shows that the contrasts led to gradual joint appreciations of the various neters. We have already referred to differences in details between the Heliopolitan and Hermopolitan traditions. While these temple centers coexisted, there is little textual material to support the existence of a creation story at Hermopolis. Indeed, texts for any myths may never have existed in the Hermopolitan tradition. However, we know that the very important moon neter and neter of wisdom, Djeuti (Thoth), originated there, while other themes and neters in the Hermopolitan tradition are depicted in images on temple walls or can be deduced from the significance and frequency of references to them in the later literature. Stories showing the character and importance of Djeuti were given in later textual materials coming from both the Heliopolitan and Memphite centers.

At the time of activity of the Heliopolitan and Hermopolitan temples in the Old Kingdom, a third important center arose at Memphis. Even in the Old Kingdom it was a major administrative center, and it persisted throughout the Middle and New Kingdoms. It eventually seems to have become the largest of Egyptian cities and perhaps was still the administrative capital of the country in the time of Plutarch (the first century CE). This center particularly emphasized creation stories concerning the neter Ptah. In later years Ptah became more important as a key figure in myths of world creation and world maintenance.

He first appeared as a mummy-wrapped being reminiscent of Osiris, standing on a slightly raised plinth, which in some cases evidently represented the original "mound" (figure 2.9). This suggests an early origin, perhaps at about the time of the Heliopolitan origin of Atum. However, this plinth symbol, or one very like it, is later also attributed to Maat, neter of justice and mate of Djeuti. Ptah was one of the two neters who took as commands and carried into action the words of the divine intelligence, Djeuti.[32] The other was Khnum, the potter of Elephantine, who modeled pharaohs on his potter's wheel (figure 2.10).

In this complex connection between neters we glimpse the genius of Egypt, which kept its mythology and religion from fragmenting into

Figure 2.9. Ptah on his plinth. Illustration by Jeff Dahl.

Figure 2.10. Khnum creating a pharaoh. In the image there are two humanoid figures, one is the pharaoh's body and the second, with arm bent, is his ka, *or spirit. From Schwaller de Lubicz,* Temple of Man, *figure 201.*

a series of unconnected cults. Thus Khnum, like Ptah, is another manifestation of the series of forms that developed from the first form, Atum, who arose from the aboriginal waters. Khnum dwelt in Heliopolis but was the lord of Elephantine, a southern town, and in later myths he was the maker of the neters and the father from the beginning. He is often shown as a man with a ram's head (figure 2.10). When shown without his potter's wheel, in one hand he holds the scepter of a pharaoh, in the other the *ankh,* the symbol of life. As Rundle Clark points out, he is represented as "a shepherd herding his flock, a Pharaoh on a throne, the idol in its shrine, as well as his past forms as lotus flower, Divine Child, hawk, serpent, ram and so on" as he developed into the High God, who shaped the pharaoh and his ka on his potter's wheel.[33]

In Hermopolis the earliest manifestations of being appeared in the form of the original Goad or the eightfold (four male neters with frog heads and four female neters with serpent heads), which flowed into one another out of the "primeval slime" to produce the primeval egg. This egg, because it contained the original "light," can be equated with Shu, the first separate being created by Atum. In strange and complex ways such as this, the myths of Heliopolis and Hermopolis became "woven together to form a background for a finally transcendent God who presides over the cosmic circuit of stars from the top of the heavenly pole," according to Rundle Clark.[34] This god, the governor of the universe, presides over this celestial axis:

> *I know his name, Eternity is his name,*
> *Eternity, the "master of years" is his name.*
> *Exalted over the vault of the sky,*
> *Bringing the sun to life every day.*[35]

Eternity and Master of Years are names for Ptah, when his being is recognized as the transcendent neter who became the High God by outgrowing the more personal designations of god in the other, earlier traditions of creation. In this quotation he is a hidden neter, an invisible source of life who presides over it from the hidden heart of the universe, most likely as a result of there being no "north star" in that position in Egyptian times.[36] He is referred to as "the greatest of those who are in the northern sky."[37] In another Pyramid Text he says:

> *I am the living soul with outstretched face*
> *Who pushed out its head, who freed itself, who brought*
> *   itself away*
> *When the doing of that which was to be done was [still]*
> *   in confusion,*
> *When the doing and the commanding of that which was*
> *   to be done was [still] asleep.*
> *I create and I command for him who commands the*
> *   good;*
> *My lips are the Twin Companies, I am the great Word,*
> *I am a redeemer—so shall I be redeemed, and I shall be*
> *   redeemed from all evil.*[38]

Here the living soul is struggling to overcome the "confusion" and "sleep" of the time of the primeval waters of Nun, but now stated more in terms of its metaphysical basis. This form of being includes all that could be seen in Atum and all his progeny, as agents of consciousness and order. But here it is of particular interest that in rousing itself from "confusion" and "sleep" the spirit, as Ptah, is a redeemer from "evil." This is explicit, additional evidence for the Egyptian belief that the spirit world is one that is above good and evil. That is, the spirit world is one in which what we call evil is experienced as "chaos" in distinction from the good that is oneness. This is seen in the later stories of Osiris, who represents the tendency toward wholeness, whereas his brother and archenemy, Seth, represents the evil that is "chaos." Evil is something that is found only in a material, fragmented lower world of nonbeing and of opposites; hence, it is a world that can be escaped only through movement into the spiritual world of order and wakefulness.

In this translation, the transformation in level from material to spiritual appears to the lower world as a change equivalent to redemption.

It is here, in this development of the Memphite theology, that we are introduced to a more active involvement of a Supreme God in all the processes of creation, even to concerns outside the immediate world of the neters themselves. (In the earlier theologies we have the sense of a rather passive development following the original awakening of Atum.) In the words of Naydler, "Ptah is the Godhead conceived as form-giver or shaper of the material world. For this reason he was also the chief neter of craftsmen and all workers in metal and stone, and was later to be identified by the Greeks as the black-smith Hephaestus. The name Ptah probably means 'sculptor' or 'engraver' and so we may picture Ptah as god at work in the [physical] world, giving to all creatures their forms."[39]

This brief summary of the various Egyptian creation myths allows us to glimpse some of the gradual melding of traditions from the various centers into a coherent and developed picture of the world. There is certainly no evidence here of any opposition among "different" schools of Egyptian mythology. There is every reason for us to see an unfolding of a world conception out of the chaos of detail. This conception meets the requirements of our modern minds. It is in the direction of the "large" scope of perception of "being." Without such development, the world of the gods can hardly appear relevant to a nearly alienated modern mindset that has been exposed to increasingly literal, moralistic, and dogmatic religious doctrines. We are faced time and again with an unsatisfactory adherence to a practical, literalistic materialism that supports the spreading of a belief and hope in science.

It is significant to the overall purpose of our study of myth that even in the time of the Egyptians there appeared a tendency to move away from what began as an almost personal view of godlike influences toward a view in which the Supreme God gradually came to exhibit more generally spiritualized characteristics that we might describe as "more than merely personal." Yet the development of the concept of god to the more than personal does not reduce the sense of the importance of being "alive," which is perhaps the main appeal of the personal in preference to the abstract.

Comparisons between Egyptian and Sumerian Creation Myths

Egyptian tales of creation show parallels with Sumerian and later Babylonian myths; even the names of some of the neters bear an associative similarity, although both became somewhat changed through time. Let's return to a consideration of the Sumerian creation myths, primarily to reflect on two features that can help us weigh the significance of differences and similarities between the Sumerian and the Egyptian points of view in relation to our interests. In what follows we start with the direct descendants of the originating Sumerian gods, An and Ki. These descendants have different names from those found in Egypt, but some of the features mentioned reveal what appear to be significant parallels. There are also contrasts, which add substance to remarks quoted earlier in this chapter from Frankfort.[40] He concludes that the myths of these two societies expressed the imperatives that led them to remarkably similar awakenings. We might expect two such societies, with their distinctive social, environmental, and behavioral environments, to show signs of independence in the more specific psychological forms. It is in our particular interest, however, to be alert to similarities or parallels that might help us define more objectively the elusive, but more ubiquitous, realm of spirituality.

As pointed out in the introduction, one of the darker areas of modern understanding lies in the difficulty we have in distinguishing what can be called the *spiritual* from the *psychological*. Clarifying this distinction is surely a major reason for undertaking this exploration of mythology. Modern studies of psychology have made known some of its more important uses in psychiatry and sociology, which for full understanding require long years of research and experience. But we know that the results of these studies and work do not readily provide the base for satisfaction in life that humankind has sought in the spiritual. Our excursion into a phenomenological study of mythology is undertaken to more clearly distinguish aspects of our personal questions that are not adequately comprehended either by modern institutionalized religion or by science. We need also to be alert to the extent to which such questions are addressed by interpretation of ancient mythical portrayals of the netherworld. We pursue this theme in chapter 6.

We will examine here parallels and differences between creation accounts given in Egyptian and Sumerian. In both, life was thought to begin by the separation of certain more active elements from the undifferentiated, primitive "sea." That is, in the primeval waters, called Nun in the Egyptian, the father of the neters became aware of himself. This first Egyptian neter then gave rise to a lineage of neters, who are presented in a hierarchy referred to as the Ennead, or nine great neters. The process of differentiation and movement within the primeval sea begins with the emergence of Tmu, who is at the head of the "great company (*pout*) of the gods"[41] and is an initial form of the great sun god, Ra.[42] In the Heliopolitan version of the creation story, Tmu is renamed Atum, "the great he/she."[43] The neter of the sky, Nut, was separated from her lover Geb, the earth neter, by Shu, who is neter of the air.

In Sumer, the original sea was known as Nammu, but it was characterized as "the Mother who gave birth to heaven and earth," without apparent concern for the subtlety of processes by which life was seen to arise from the inanimate in Egypt.[44] Questions about how life arises outside of materiality, or breaks free from roots in materiality, seem to be entirely side-stepped in the Sumerian myths, as are any questions about the mechanism through which new beings are created from the original "One." The impression we get from the Egyptian story of a careful and thoughtful, to us even somewhat internalized, esoteric view of the processes involved in the creation mystery seems far less evident than from the Sumerian version. What is recorded in the Sumerian account could be described as simple, externalized statements. Do they reflect a superficially utilitarian approach? Or is there reason to search more deeply into them?

There are apparent parallels among the characteristics of some of the subsequent generations of the gods of the two societies. For example, as in Egypt, earth and heaven were actively separated out of an initial unity in the Sumerian and Babylonian creation stories. The brief passages quoted tell that An, the father of the gods, had taken heaven, while the god Enlil, one of An's sons (or grandsons?) had taken earth. Thus, it is of more than incidental interest that the two syllables of Enlil's name literally mean "god" and "breath," "air," or "wind." In effect, the god responsible for taking the earth seems to be presented in much the same position as the Egyptian Shu.

This may indicate a similar background of influences at some point in the past. Yet the characters demonstrated by the bearers of the names Enlil and Shu, the orientation and significance of their actions, and their subsequent roles in their respective worlds have such a different flavor that attributing similarity to them would be artificially forced. We cannot justify more than a possible vaguely remembered common initial impulse on this account. We also note in the Sumerian quotation on page 27 that the goddess Ereshkigal is given the netherworld as a gift, but that event is not mentioned in the Babylonian version. We have not identified a comparable individual in an Egyptian neter. We shall examine her attributes and their significance more closely in our consideration of the Duat in chapter 6.

Enki and Djeuti

Continuing pursuit of our question about the "agents" of the creation of the world, let us now compare the characters of another of the principal gods of Sumer and his nearest Egyptian parallel. We have in mind comparing the principal Sumerian god, named Enki, with the important Egyptian neter Djeuti, who is much better known by his Greek name, Thoth. Both of them have been called gods of wisdom in their respective literatures, so a comparison should at least help us understand possible differences in the meaning of the word *wisdom*. Enki's name is evidently a compound of the word *en,* meaning "god" or "heaven," or perhaps "divine," and *ki,* meaning "earth" or "mother," a term that suggests a being with powers that extended over aspects in both the spiritual and material jurisdictions. Enki is, indeed, one of the most interesting and subtle of all Sumerian gods, responsible for many practical matters but also sensitive to the more emotional needs of his "subjects," both lesser gods and humankind.

Djeuti, whose Egyptian name means "the measurer," is a similarly complex neter, with unspecified parentage.[45] He is credited with making the calculations for the establishment of the heavens, stars, earth, and everything in them.[46] He is said to have invented hieroglyphic writing. His initial appearance is in the Hermopolitan tradition, where he is described as a high neter whose "divine intelligence" uttered the "words" of creation that were then carried out by Ptah and Khnum, both of whom were later also assigned the status of "high gods." Whatever his exact origin, his designation as a neter of wisdom and justice is supported by many of his small acts. For example, one of his modes of behavior was to observe the actions of younger neters with particular care and, where appropriate, rectify the wrong results of impulsive actions. He was also a moon neter, further suggesting a subtlety of emotional relations.

Both Djeuti and Enki were neters of wide understanding who carried out their perceptions of right action primarily through the use of "the word," rather than through direct intervention or action. We are confident that in this case the parallels reflect a common understanding of the needs for care, patience, and sympathy as important aspects of the power that we expect to be exercised by superior gods, those having "divine intelligence." In one sense we can contrast Enki with Enlil, who was vastly superior to all other Sumerian gods in terms of power. But in this distinction we are offered a glimpse of the actual breadth of the Sumerian sensitivity. In these two Sumerian "gods" or "principles" we find a deliberate contrast between power and intelligence, especially that aspect we will deal with in chapter 5 called "intelligence of the heart." It is a characteristic important enough to have been carried as a main theme into Christianity, which is held to have begun through revelation two thousand years later.

Another aspect of Enki's character and sense of responsibility is revealed in one of the chief Sumerian myths that tell of the creation of the material and organic world. Kramer gives the first English translation, titled "Enki and the World Order." It begins with praises to Enki as the god who "watches over the universe and is responsible for the fertility of field and farm, of flock and herd."[47] He is praised for ensuring the prosperity and abundance of the earth, and in the course of the poem arranges for the provision of everything from minerals, such as gold, tin, and bronze, to reeds and trees, green vegetation that supplies food for all the grazing animals, fish for fish ponds, and all that is needed for their continued fertility and abundant production. He completes the exhibition of his wisdom and munificence by ensuring that the Tigris and Euphrates are properly regulated, providing for life-giving rain, and establishing the fertility of the sea for the use of humankind. In each case he ensures the continued prosperity and abundance of all the good things created by appointing various minor gods to oversee them, including the assignment of several of the lesser gods whose first responsibility was to Enlil.

The exhaustive account of Enki's responsibilities leaves no doubt that he oversaw the maintenance of the material world of humankind. In this way he parallels a number of the characteristics of the Egyptian god Osiris, in that Osiris, in company with his sister-wife, Isis, originally taught humankind agricultural practices and implements, cooking, weaving, and the making of wine and beer, and also ensured the renewal of vegetative growth following the season of heat and drought. Both accounts seem exhaustive in their consideration of what humankind's material needs were and how they could best be organized and assured. Both appear to directly address humankind's questions about how the practical aspects of civilization began and how the gods play an appropriate role in its maintenance. There seems to be no special reason for surprise that the attention of the gods should be lavished on living beings in various, more or less parallel ways in the two traditions. However, we note that this Sumerian record still does not address the question of how humans are related to the gods and the spiritual world in terms of the nonmaterial qualities that are of interest to us.

Three Sumerian myths lend insight into how their view of the maintenance of creation differed from the Egyptian view. The first myth concerns the creation of men and women, and this was given only in the introduction to a longer myth. It is described by Kramer but not given a title. The theme was taken up in somewhat different form in *The Babylonian Genesis* and in the other Babylonian myths introduced at the start of this chapter. However, the creation of men and women is not given specific treatment at all in Egyptian mythology, nor is it elaborated further in the Sumerian mythos beyond these fragments. The other two Sumerian myths include a repeated, extensive, and unique listing of heterogeneous qualities, called the "Arts of Civilization," or *mes* in Sumerian. These mes, which may be considered values or mores, were essential for maintaining organizational relations among the human social groups in Sumer and for mediating human relations with the gods.

The Sumerian Creation of Men and Women

Themes concerning the relations between humans and gods on the level of "moral" responsibility, granted by god to humans, such as is taught in the Ten Commandments, can also be found in the writings of the Egyptians and Sumerians. They appear in the Sumerian story of Gilgamesh, who was king of the ancient city of Ur, an early capital of Sumer. He is said in the myth to be two-thirds god and one-third man, so his relations with the gods are an essential part of that story. In this chapter we direct our attention to the creation of humans in the

Sumerian myths, which appears as an almost incidental reference. The Sumerians seem not to have been constrained to the spiritual to the extent that the Egyptians were. It must be recognized that there was a transition from the Sumerian concept of creation to that captured in the Babylonian mythology of 1,000 years later. It is the later Babylonian mythology that has colored much of the subsequent modern Western mindset.

In the Sumerian accounts, the creation of men and women is explained only in the introduction to a myth that is not named but is described and discussed by Kramer.[48] A parallel although less directly stated version is given as part of another Sumerian myth, titled "Enki and Nimah" and translated in the ETCSL.[49] Both begin with the statement that the gods were having difficulty in procuring bread to eat. Enki, the god of wisdom who would have been able to help, was then apparently asleep in the deep and did not hear their protests and complaints. So Nammu, the goddess of the primeval sea and mother of all the gods, had to waken him and solicit his help to fashion "servants of the gods."[50] On being approached, Enki immediately appreciated the need, and after giving the matter "thought," says:

> *Oh my Mother! The creature whose name you uttered,*
> > *it exists.*
> *Bind upon it the image of the gods.*
> *Mix the heart of the clay that is over the abyss.*
> *The good and princely fashioners will thicken the clay,*
> *You! Do you bring the limbs into existence?*
> *Nimah (the earth-mother goddess) will work above you,*
> *(goddess of birth) . . . will stand by you at the*
> > *fashioning;*
> *Oh my Mother! Decree its fate,*
> *Nimah will bind upon it the mould of the gods,*
> *It is man. . . .*[51]

This part of the story ends here, and the myth takes up a different story, in which Enki has organized a feast. During the festivities, Enki and Nimah drink too much beer, and Nimah claims that her will should enable her to create humans. The result is a failure, producing defective beings. The purpose served by this further story was initially somewhat obscure, but readable parts of the recent retranslation suggest that it showed that Nimah's limitations needed to be supplemented by interaction with Enki's level of understanding. The last line reads, "Nimah could not rival the great lord Enki. Father Enki, your praise is sweet."[52] With this brief statement this addendum to the creation story is terminated.

One aspect that we wish to note in this Sumerian account is the statement that "clay" is the substance from which humans are created. Under Enki's direction and to help the gods with this newly perceived need, the goddess Ninhursag, or Ki, undertakes this initiative. Humans are created from clay to serve the gods.

The Sumerian Organization of Society

In two epic poems—one describing Enki's responsibility for creating the plants and animals of Sumer titled "Enki and the World Order"[53] and the other describing civilizing influences, titled "Inanna and Enki: The Transfer of the Arts of Civilization from Eridu to Erech"[54]—the list of more than one hundred characteristics that guided the mores of society, or mes, is repeated several times. This list shows, among other things, how certain of the valued attitudes and behaviors may at times appear to be quite contradictory. It therefore provides us with additional insights into the maintenance of organizational relations, as well as into the nature of their concerns.[55]

The list of more than one hundred features demonstrates that ensemble living was originally the responsibility of Enki, when he was designated as the chief "god" of the earthly organization. Some of these features were taken over by the "goddess of love and war," Inanna, by trickery, which is not of special concern to us here—it was eventually returned to the appropriate guardian.* They are listed in a generally descending order from the higher, more-than-personal to the personal. But we can review highlights by naming the qualities, "arts," or mes that are most clearly legible on the clay tablets—given here as far as possible in the order in which they appear in Kramer's original, with some of the descriptive words amended after consultation with the versions edited by ETCSL.

1. Enship; 2. Godship; 3. The exalted and enduring crown; 4. The throne of kingship; 5. The exalted sceptre; 6. The royal insignia; 7. The exalted shrine; 8. Shepherdship; 9. Kingship; 10–14. Various priestess and priestly offices; 15. Truth; 16. Descent into the netherworld [kur]; 17. Ascent from the netherworld [kur]; 18–20. [attributes of functions of eunuchs?]; 21. The battle standard; 22. The flood; 23. Weapons; 24. Sexual intercourse; 25. Prostitution; 26. Law (?); 27. Libel (?); 28. Art; 29. The cult chamber; 30. "hierodule of heaven"; 31. Guslim (a musical instrument); 32. Music; 33. Eldership; 34. Heroship; 35. Power; 36. Enmity; 37. Straightforwardness; 38. The destruction of cities; 39. Lamentation; 40. Rejoicing of the heart; 41. Falsehood; 42–47. Various crafts including: metalworking, smith, scribeship, leatherwork, builder, basket weaver . . . ; 48. Wisdom; 49. Attention; 50. Holy purification; 51. Fear; 52. Terror; 53. Strife; 54. Peace; 55. Weariness . . .[56]

Kramer points out that this list of mes occurs four times in the "Inana and Enki" myth alone, and therefore it must have been regarded by the Sumerians as a most valuable teaching and guidance tool. This list offers ample evidence of a perception of the relative values of a varied set of objects, acts, and attitudes. Overall it displays little concern with differences among individual "principles," but it clearly directs

---

*The end of this myth, as given in the ETCSL, implies that Enki did eventually get the stewardship of the mes back from Inanna, but not without a considerable struggle!

attention to hierarchical differences in the status of particular qualities of behavior that can be attributed to the various occupations of human-kind. It implies that the Sumerians gave attention to levels of sensitivity to higher emotional qualities in individual and social lives. It is notable that they realistically include what we would term both negative and positive emotional attitudes.

Several examples may be worth special consideration in illustrating the level of sensitivity to which the Sumerians aspired. The list begins with the term *Enship,* apparently a high priestly office that is distinguished from *Godship.* This is a distinction that may be almost lost on us, except for the realization that in our time we distinguish a term of general significance of a given property from those terms that describe specific examples. Consider the difference in significance between *the spiritual* and *the divine* and various levels of perception that we would attribute to "god." Such a distinction made in this context gives us, at the very least, a hint of the discernment exhibited in the Sumerian storytelling. In this way we might appreciate that such storytelling is appealing to our own best levels of discrimination among those values that have greatest significance for us.

Similar attention can be usefully directed to other items in the list. Many of the general properties of kingship are represented as *"The exalted and enduring crown," "The throne of kingship," "The exalted sceptre," "The royal insignia,"* and *"Kingship"* itself. It is curious to note that *"Shepherdship"* is mixed into the order of kingly characteristics and comes before *"Kingship"* in the listing. This exhibits a level of subtlety in distinguishing qualities beyond the purely physical to the higher qualities such as the spiritual. This list, which was written on clay tablets about 4,500 years ago, presents us with evidence of a level of discrimination that far exceeds generalizations that we might have reached from more casual readings of ancient Sumerian literature.

We can only add that the appearance of such a list assures us of the high regard in which the Sumerians looked at the potential of human life, and additionally gives us an expression of the faith that they had in the ability of their auditors to hear and learn. It is a remarkable testimonial to the culture's social interaction, development, and intelligence, and these attributes well justify a study of their myths.

This simple list shows that at the social level of humankind, the Sumerians clearly appreciated that there is a responsibility on the part of individuals. The list provides a sense of the accommodation or reconciliation required among the conflicting emotions that appear in our daily lives. The list also indicates the ability of humans to appreciate and, where possible, assist in conditions that contribute to reconciliation. The listing includes many qualities that in Egypt are classed as principles assigned to the purview of particular neters. Here there is no suggestion that such qualities needed to be under the specific guardianship of a god, and yet we note that the Sumerians attributed the original keeping of this list to the god Enki. We cannot but agree that this seems very much in keeping with the degree of stewardship that we have learned to associate with Enki. Such was made clear in our earlier comparative study of the characteristics of Enki and Djeuti, or Thoth.

In these Sumerian myths, in a number of instances, mischievous or drunken behavior is also attributed to the gods, factors that were certainly taken into account in the later Greek myths. In later, New Kingdom Egyptian stories, there is an extended satire of the original myth of Osiris in the well-known tale of the major struggle between Horus and Seth. In it, there is a description of behavior of gods that varies from the preposterous and ridiculous to the obscene and blasphemous. Again, the overriding intention seems to be an entertaining story, based on perceived obvious contradictions between the behaviors of both gods and humans. But while we ourselves need to remain open to the idea of a reconciliation of opposites, these displays of unexpectedly "lower" behavior among the gods in both the Sumerian and Egyptian examples may even have been intended to invoke an additional sense of perspective through humor. They might also invite disbelief. Or they could be interpreted as intentionally conveying the impression of a superficial, hence unsatisfying, level of penetration into the psyche of humans or gods that invites a deeper contemplation by the auditors.

Some of the mes seem intended to point to problems that will arise between participants in human societies, at all levels. Others are definitely pointing to higher levels of development. They are certainly associated with the godlike, primarily as an understandable generalization of the human. However, we need to remember where we began our search. How do we arrive at perceptions of a higher state that can only be dimly perceived and aspired to from the lower levels of human action? It is clearly recognized that it is often difficult for human individuals to see themselves, their own personal habits and attitudes. This list of mes shows evidence of the Sumerian awareness of such problems. Whether we think in terms of humans or gods, we are sometimes forced, but at other times led more voluntarily, to find in them evidence for a consideration of difficult questions of the meaning of life. To quote Frye, "at times of special insight on our own parts we may be led, as with particularly fine music, into recognizing the essence of the problems we are confronting," hence of the values about which we are able to raise questions.[57] We tentatively conclude that we have in these instances examples of essential values that may help us define by both similarity and difference the nature of the spiritual, rather than the strictly psychological.

The Babylonian Revision of the Sumerian Creation of Humankind

Following the Akkadian conquest, the Sumerian originals were gradually neglected and lost and had virtually disappeared before the second millennium BCE, until Middle East excavations and explorations exposed them once again during the mid-nineteenth century CE. But the core concepts persisted.

In the foregoing Sumerian creation of men and women, we noted that the humans get very little attention in the main stories. The same is not true for the Babylonian versions that purport to deal with the same themes. A later and unexpectedly altered version occurs in the

Babylonian myths cited by Heidel and deserves our attention partly because of what appear to be still unappreciated consequences of this later "invention."[58] The Babylonian myths are essentially stories that were intended to glorify the Babylonian god Marduk. This building of a new myth on the traditionally known Sumerian stories took place following the conquest of the Sumerian regions by Semitic tribes, beginning under Sargon I of Akkad around 2250 BCE and completed under the Babylonian Hammurabi some five hundred years later. It is the later Babylonian stories that were picked up by the Hebrews, who passed them on to both Christians and Muslims. We need to be alert to the possibility that the various cultures that adopted these stories promoted them for different reasons. The reasons for mythmaking radically changed over the centuries. The politics of power became evident as the chief motive in later times. Not that changes had not appeared earlier, nor that they do not still appear in mythmaking. We have to be careful to discuss politically and economically motivated themes separately from serious questions about the nature of the universe and the place of gods and humans in it. We have earlier adopted this as the principal reason for our study of myths!

The evidence that myths were used to influence religious beliefs as an aspect of political dominance appears particularly clear here in the treatment by the Babylonians. The process of gradually building on the Sumerian mythology apparently began around the time the name Enki was changed to Ea. A more obviously important change occurs with the creation of the new god, Marduk. He was a son of Ea who later became much greater than his father; through Marduk additional feats became possible.[59] Also, humans were no longer described as being made of clay, but now they were created out of the blood of an evil deity, Kingu, whom the other gods identified and slew! Marduk's followers presented his blood to Ea so that he could create humans according to an inspirational plan attributed to Marduk.

The intended purpose of this "twist" in the myth of creation by the Babylonians is obscure, but we note it here because of what may be unexpected consequences. The change, from clay to the blood of an evil god, implies that from the start humankind was created with character-istics of "evil" that set them apart from the gods, who had not shared in the evil attributed to the slain god. Kingu had been an associate of the turbulent original goddess Tiamat, goddess of saltwater and the mate of Anu, original Babylonian god of all creation and lord of the freshwater of the abyss. That is, Kingu was allied with primal, though not neces-sarily evil, powers.

This factor is important because much of this version of the cre-ation story was adopted by the Hebrews, who were captive in Babylon at the time, and passed on to Christianity. The goddess Tiamat shows up only in the Akkadian and Babylonian myths. Initially it is she and Anu who occupy themselves with the creation of gods, as did An and Ki in the Sumerian tales. However, in the Babylonian version, when Anu and Tiamat grew older they became impatient with the multitude of younger gods, who finally made such a noise with their partying that the old gods could not sleep. Anu was so bothered that he decided to kill them so that all would again be quiet, as it had previously been.[60] Tiamat didn't like the idea of killing their own line of progeny. But Anu made plans anyway; however, his plans became known to the young gods, who were highly surprised and upset. They appealed to Ea, who agreed to help. Then, by uttering magic words, Ea put a "spiri-tual" shield around the younger gods to protect them and proceeded to cast another spell that put Anu to sleep. He then slew the great god Anu, completely removing the threat! This whole process relieved the immediate threat so that the shield could be removed from around the younger gods.

The act did not immediately clarify the difficulties by bringing the situation to an immediate end. The upset state of affairs was used by the Babylonian mythmakers to justify a great struggle arising between Marduk, son of Ea, and the resentful ancient goddess Tiamat. (Marduk was in the process of being made into the principal god of Babylon.) Using elaborate and dramatic terminology, the tale tells then how

Tiamat led a ferocious band of monsters against the Babylonian gods, which caused Marduk to save them (hence the kingdom) by slaying Tiamat, whose remains were then used to form parts of the material world. The lesser gods, who were termed Annunaki and Igigi, completed the job by slaying the evil god Kingu, who had been a lieutenant of Tiamat, and gave his blood to Ea so that he could use it to create humans.

This confusion of motives, including the strange concept of the killing of heretofore immortal gods, including the great god Anu, was apparently utilized to adapt the Sumerian creation myth into a paean of praise for Marduk. But we are left with the ironic situation that this bald political motivation may have been responsible for introducing the idea of the fundamentally evil nature of humans into the Babylonian myth of creation. Is this how the idea of a basically evil nature for humans entered into early Christian ideas?

These transformations of Sumerian myth into their Babylonian "equivalents" introduce an even more important, if inadvertent, development. We are hereby crediting the Babylonians with the first explicit expression of psychological motives in mythmaking, distinctly different from the spiritual motives that appear to have influenced the Sumerians. This kind of discovery has been part of the reason for our search through these ancient creation myths. It seems serendipitous to have detected it in the move away from the original Sumerian myth, but such a discovery is a byproduct of our resolve to keep as close as possible to the essence of the originals.

The Egyptian Creation of Men and Women

We are so accustomed through Western traditions to expecting that the origin and fate of humankind must be the ultimate focus of ancient mythology that it comes as something of a shock to realize that there is no particular Egyptian origin myth in which the creation of men and women is the prime focus. In fact, according to the Egyptian myths, creation is entirely concerned with a metaphysical cosmos. Until we hear of Ptah's interventions, humans do not even enter into consideration in the Egyptian world until after their death. The whole focus of Egyptian interest was on the spiritual, not the material world. It would then be naive of us to expect among the Egyptians an account of the transformation of the physical into the spiritual, in parallel with what is considered to be the relevant route to what is higher in our society. Egyptian mythology holds that our life originates from the higher levels of consciousness; the lower levels in which we live only came about afterward. In the case of the ancient Egyptians, the distinction between physical and spiritual life is of significance only as they affect the well-being of the spiritual world. The connection between the physical and metaphysical worlds for the Egyptians appears in the later phases of the myths, which address the relationships between gods and humans. These arise in the context of the myths of Osiris that we deal with later in chapter 5.

Summary

Our probing is inevitably conditioned by expectations and interests based on our own individual histories. Yet we remain aware that these have been conditioned in unsuspected ways by the values of the societies around us and preceding us. For this reason it may be appropriate to make an explicit summary of what we perceive to be the most important points discussed in this chapter, and to make some projections about what we believe is needed for proceeding along the path of study of myth.

We have attempted to show that both the Sumerian and Egyptian traditions focus on the metaphysical creation of the world of the gods, not the physical world in which humanity lives. They are concerned with spiritual creation, that is, the awakening of higher consciousness, or of godlike traits, within a usually undifferentiated awareness.

The early myths of both Sumer and Ancient Egypt inserted into a conception of creation the necessity for undifferentiated "waters" to contain something in which a new and different state appears, one out of which the gods make their appearance. The arising of the first god implies the appearance of a sense of higher consciousness within this preexisting, primeval sea. We understand this in an esoteric way; this creation is not the creation of a material world but an esoteric internal awakening of higher consciousness.

Creation myths from the Middle and Near East are in accord in another respect as well. They imply that our questions about the ultimate origin of life are asking for more than a simple statement about a "sense of being" that arises "spontaneously" from a preexistent metaphysical materiality. The creators of these early myths recognized—and we do as well—a need for something more, perhaps something comparable to the difference between the impression made by the mysterious stars moving silently in the vast night sky and the impression created by the formless and endless blackness of the night sky against which they move. What we require may not actually be "thought out." It may be an instinctive response that leads us to question what current "reason" tells us and to persist in our sense of wonder at an inanimate substance that, through a creative act, makes life possible, with its unique properties of movement and sensitivity. The simple act of discriminating between the esoteric and the exoteric is our first step away from the initial undifferentiated unity.

We also need to recognize complexities in what the ancients saw as the properties of "number." In creation stories we are clearly treading near the edges of the nature of thought and the power of the processes of thinking. The subject of number raises important questions—see appendix 3. Both West[61] and R. A. Schwaller de Lubicz[62] point to our need to recognize that the initial arising of life and consciousness involve the transition of oneness, or wholeness—the universality of the undifferentiated Great Ocean—into the essential new condition of duality. R. A. Schwaller de Lubicz's book *The Temple of Man* presents another mode of thinking, one distinguished from the ordinary analytical mind. It introduces a mode that puts form to the fore, emphasizing the "heart" in contrast to the "mind." The difference may be between intuition and thinking, or between induction and deduction. Surely the interaction between two different ways of thinking is the essence of myth itself.

If we accept the view of the ancient Egyptians that it is impossible to explain creation as the appearance of the quality of twoness from the splitting of a unique one, we recognize that in creation there must be a mysterious additional process involved for the coming into being of a sense of "life" out of the unitary void. The change is comparable, within a given individual, to coming from a deep sleep into a state of wakefulness. This general distinction is implied in all the creation myths and is made quite explicit in the Egyptian myth of the stirring into awareness of Atum. This distinction naturally leads us to consider how such a differentiated state can be manifested in the physical world, what we think of as the "real" world.

The early descriptions of a spiritual beginning, instead of invoking the difficult concept of "nothing," entertained the concept of "undifferentiated waters." For us the term *undifferentiated waters* may suggest a substance, which can lead us to questions of "form." But Sumerian and Egyptian creation texts, as well as the later Christian stories, avoid an initial specification of form. The modern Christian account begins with a concept of "God," a capacity for being that is before anything else, unlimited, formless, and undifferentiated.

We need to exercise awareness of the differences between the levels of consciousness embodied in mythical language and those associated with existence in the ordinary world. Even this quick, superficial comparison between the Sumerian and Egyptian views of creation highlights the need to carefully attend to the level of attention within ourselves when studying myth. As we delve further into the myths, we need to be clear about our motives for making such comparisons.

We can say, initially, that it is obvious the Sumerian and ancient Egyptian societies producing these myths perceived our world as consisting of at least two distinct levels of existence, which are clearly identified as "above" and "below." It is also clear that, as we expect from myths, these two names do not "delimit" these domains, they simply indicate the existence of two levels that can be perceived objectively by an observer who finds and maintains a position intermediate between them, rather than in one or the other. What is less clear is the nature of the beings, called gods, that can be seen as personifications of our internal world. In both cases these gods appear to be a kind of personification of "principles" that guide our own external and interior behaviors and attitudes as human beings. The myths clearly give rise to both exoteric stories of development and esoteric reflections of insight.

The lack of identifying detail, in other than the names given these different levels, may be intentional, to allow our natural mental processes to find an equivalence for levels of existence in the "actual" world of our own impressions and emotions. It is implied that differences in the characteristics of these levels also underlie the relationships we can recognize within and among them.

The comparison between the myths of these two societies then helps us question the significance of differences between the two conceptions of gods or principles that are suggested to us. For example, we have noted differences in the interactions that underlie the stories. There is an emphasis in the Sumerian stories on struggles, amounting at times to violence, among the gods. We interpret this as reflecting an attitude that developed during the organization of the society that tells stories of these gods. This point of view is verified when the Sumerian myths were replaced by the Babylonian stories. Their similarity to interactions we have already learned to expect from the human beings of subsequent periods, such as war and conquest, up to and including our own, seems too clear to be passed over without this specific mention.

In contrast, we have noted a more direct concern of both the Sumerian and Egyptian myths with the world that is outside the ordinary. These stories are more evidently oriented toward what might take place before birth and after death than with the concerns that affect human behavior during our social and individual lives. On closer inspection it may in fact be true that the social organization of the Sumerian peoples into city-states, as opposed to the organization into interdependent states in Egypt, resulted in a significant difference in outlook between them, especially when it concerns the way they lived.

It must be admitted that expectations of difference, reflected in such early comparisons as were made by Frankfort, may place too much emphasis on the significance of the social milieu.[63] This was characteristic of our society in the earlier part of the twentieth century. There is certainly a difference between the societies that reflects their unique personalities. The Egyptian myths are more introspective and show esoteric concern with human perceptions of what is valuable. The Sumerian myths are somewhat more oriented toward an exoteric, perhaps extroverted, view of the interactions of the beings called gods, in their "incarnations" as physical beings. However, when we inspect the "values" represented in the list of mes that are found in the Sumerian myths, such values can also be recognized in the Egyptian writings as describing phenomena important in both societies. Thus any distinctions seem far less evident.

Do we have here another, perhaps even more significant reason for finding a fundamental similarity between the two societies? The Egyptians seem to have identified detailed aspects of spiritual life showing great discrimination between levels of being. Such discrimination is well beyond what might be expected of a primitive society based on "magic spells." And while the Sumerian hymns and myths lack a clear distinction between the behavior or responsibilities of humans and gods, they do hint at moments of tenderness and of qualities of interaction in the direction of enduring values, such as spirituality.

In both the Sumerian and Egyptian myths, there is an overriding concern with the definition of enduring and common human values—values that transcend individual preferences and demonstrate superior perception. Such values have an ineffable quality that might be described as more "spiritual" than "psychological." We conclude that the myths do not enable us to clearly define what we mean by the term *spiritual,* yet we can at the same time appreciate an ability to communicate about them on the basis of our personal experiences in relationship, in both serious and lighter modes. We conclude that our personal searches for an approach to the meaning of life might be further clarified in myths that are beyond the class of creation myths. We undertake a pursuit of these other kinds of myths in the following chapters.

THREE

A DIALOGUE OF THE AGES

The experience of awakening higher consciousness within us is as old as the stories of the gods. The fact that the concept is rarely considered in our time is a sobering reminder of how limited the approach of Western culture has been to the difficult questions of reality. In our time we seem confined to differentiating between the dichotomy of "reality" and "illusion." Those interested in questions of reality therefore must endeavor to reestablish a fully dimensional perceptual world to provide a context for the wisdom that is embedded in ancient myths. Despite one's impulses to take action that could remedy this situation, history shows that our natures are not readily open to the required sense of order, even when we believe the undertaking to be of great importance. However, it is sometimes seen, in studying one's direct experiences, that our personal impulses to take action can cooperate in creating a requisite level of being.

That special part of our natures that connects with the requisite level of being is spiritual. Spiritual nature is continually opposed by the illusory. We seem adrift in a sea of uncertainty that suggests that this area of our nature has its own illusions. The solid ground of reality is clearly not easy to discover. The desire to clarify our wish for this higher consciousness is the main reason for studying ancient myths. The important objective for readers is awakening to see the illusory world in which we live our daily lives.

One of the oldest and best known of the Hebrew myths deals precisely with this important question. The story of Adam and Eve contained in the second and third chapters of the book of Genesis in the Old Testament can be seen to relate to the story of the creation of humankind. But in paying special attention to the translation of this passage, we may discern certain lessons about what constitutes illusion and what is the nature of true knowledge.

The Kabbalistic studies of the Hebrew texts specify four levels of interpretation: literal, allegorical, moral, and esoteric. We prefer to use the term hieroglyphic rather than moral. This is similar to R. A. Schwaller de Lubicz's concept of the symbolique (*Symbol and the Symbolic*). The story of Adam and Eve in the Garden of Eden can be viewed with these four levels in mind. While many interpretations scarcely go beyond the literal, there can be little doubt of the great possibilities the story offers as symbolism, and many books have been written in explanation of one view or another. It is an important and familiar example of an ancient myth and is, therefore, an appropriate place to test our perceptions.

French author, poet, and composer d'Olivet (1767–1825) interpreted the story of the Garden of Eden in *The Hebraic Tongue Restored*.[1] The Garden of Eden story directly follows the principal Hebrew myth of the creation of the world, thus implying questions about the place of humans in this creation. At a literal level these passages can be taken simply as a description of the creation of physical bodies, such as the planets (figure 3.1 on page 72), but the Sumerian and Egyptians myths previously discussed remind us that the myths are concerned with an esoteric process of creation of our inner selves. Only through a process of self-creation or opening are we able to undertake a deeper inquiry into the meanings of our experiences in the world. Through mythology, readers of this book should be able to distinguish between the "institutional" renderings commonly encountered in the everyday world and the point of view that we have been undertaking in our explorations in this book.

In the following passages we undertake an experiment in using dialogue. From the Upanishads of India to the dialogues of Plato, a most important ancient literary vehicle for conveying the meaning and flavor of philosophical stories that were once recited to audiences has been the presentation of their content in the form of conversations between a pupil and teacher. This device allows the reader a measure of objectivity in the point of view of the story that may not appear in a more direct confrontation between reader and writer. We therefore propose to listen in on a conversation between two friends who, because of their celestial stature, communicate over a span of especially large geographies and times. In addition, because of differences in their "ages," they bring different perspectives to the exchange of esoteric knowledge.

A Conversation between Friends

Aquarius crossed the star garden and seated himself near his aging friend Pisces. Pisces felt the younger individual's presence, and a more relaxed breathing filled his aging frame. A few moments passed before the younger man broke the easy silence.

"I have looked at the Hebrew stories of which you spoke," Aquarius said, "and I need to ask you about the questions they have aroused in me. I understand that the God who created humankind must introduce his creation, Adam, to the laws of the universe, but some of these seem to be merely restrictions of Adam's freedom for which I cannot see the reason. Because he is created an individual, do the stories intend to point out his need to develop a sense of responsibility for his own actions?

"I also see that all of the living beings he meets in the garden must have been influenced by forces acting at many different levels. But what is this figure the story calls the snake? I don't understand it or why it speaks to Eve rather than Adam. How in this incident is Adam

Figure 3.1. Jupiter as seen through the pillars of the Hypostyle Hall in the Luxor Temple, Egypt.

related to her actions? Is he just an innocent bystander who unwittingly agreed to bite forbidden fruit? And why should the fruit of the Tree of Knowledge be forbidden anyway? How could a genuine knowledge of good and evil bring shame and fear?

"I don't understand how what is called 'the fall' could be considered a fall from grace. Why was it not just an awakening awareness of their newly created state of being alive? I have to ask myself if they were so ignorant of their underlying animal natures that they could not accept they would have urges that would be felt at various levels within themselves. Is there something missing in their natures that is being hinted at, but is not yet known by them without special help?"

Aquarius continued, "I see hints of a deeper meaning in these stories, but many of the images are so indistinct that it is difficult to understand them. Apparently their power to evoke understanding is so strong that they have been preserved from the beginning of the time of Aries; perhaps Moses even took them from an earlier teaching! But they raise more questions than answers for me. Is it possible for me to comprehend what is contained in them? Or are the meanings deliberately hidden from us? Could I learn to make such stories my own?"

Pisces smiled. In the brief overlap of their lives he had been able to taste youth again in the intensity of his young friend's desire to get directly to the heart of questions. He had also glimpsed the signs of insight that spoke of new possibilities. He found reason for hope in his friend's openness.

"You have begun a most difficult inquiry," Pisces said. "I recall that you've told me many times how you have seen that new understanding depends on a special relation between what is perceived as coming from without and what lies within. Real perceptions pass so quickly! I am sure that the insights you seek can be found, but they require great patience and effort.

"At the same time, you are right to be wary that original meanings may be buried or obscured. This often happens in repeated transcriptions and translations, and may be unintentional. Those who wrote down and those who translated the Hebrew in the accounts that are known today were as constrained by their own times and experiences as we are. Even so, we need to be on our guard against reading them in an ordinary way. It is necessary to search oneself for meaning as thoroughly as one searches the texts. Meanings at first hard to discern are often invitations to special efforts of pondering. The results of the efforts show better than anything else whether the old texts have remained true to the original intentions."

Pisces' remarks led Aquarius to recall the joy of discovery he had found in moments of earlier learning, but the sense of again being surrounded by invisible barriers was strong. He felt caught and unable to respond to the urge to reach out and grasp something new. "When I try the hardest to approach these ideas, they seem the most elusive," he replied. "They continually slip beyond my grasp! They almost seem to mock my efforts to capture a new idea.

"I know that when the new perceptions arise they are not really 'mine,' but they are something in which I participate," Aquarius continued. "And it is true that a sense of sharing in them does not arise at all unless I have been trying. And so the feeling that I must try harder arises despite my best wishes. The paradox I see is that this trying harder creates tensions that continually pull me away from my intentions to be open to the images!"

"Yes," answered Pisces. "When this happens to us we feel sympathy for Tantalus, eternally punished in Tartarus. His conditions were more like ours than we like to think. He was prevented from satisfying his hunger or thirst, and continually reminded of the impossibility of grasping objects that seemed so close at hand. Even after repeated trying we are sometimes unable to satisfy our desires, let alone our real needs. Yet, even without the power to change our circumstances by ourselves there is still within us a sense of other possible approaches, perhaps even the path of learning how to remove ourselves from desires!

"There seems to me to be a kind of magnetism in our world that helps to orient our efforts," continued Pisces. "With patience and the determination to relax and be open to the present, opportunity arises. This state may enable us to learn how to use the help that is offered to us."

"I have experienced something like that in the past," said Aquarius with visible relaxation. "But how do I address this strong feeling that something of great importance calls to me, and yet I do not know how to approach it?"

"I believe we need to accept that there may be an order in our learning that perhaps cannot be seen except with help," replied Pisces. "But it is difficult for us. Being helped depends on influences that are not obvious. In part it even depends on finding the right material at the right time.

"There is a lawful sequence in which important ideas can be assimilated, and that sequence was expressed in tales that belong to a long tradition. Perhaps it is useful to realize that the Hebrew texts from the Age of Aries echo even older sacred writings of the ancient Egyptians in the Age of Taurus. According to ancient knowledge, not only the stories but also the words themselves have been constructed with such care that where the originals are still accessible, the meanings intentionally placed in them long ago can still help us reach new levels of understanding.

"The method used by the ancients allowed for the transmission of thoughts of the most subtle nature by the important device of drawing on the inner knowledge of the inquirer. As can be seen in the Egyptian hieroglyphs and ancient Hebrew, each glyph, like the words themselves, stands for a concept that we need to understand at different levels of interpretation: literal, allegorical, hieroglyphic, even esoteric! The concepts at each level are in turn linked with others to form a new concept that embodies the parts, yet is greater than their simple sum. It is said that the positions of the glyphs in relation to each other, both their order and their interaction, also impart meaning.

"While it sounds complicated when it is described in this way, there is actually a simplicity and directness about the technique, provided the reader understands the invitation to participate in the story. It is a very old technique, strongly related to the oral traditions that are so rare now. Its simplicity allows subtlety and exactness without the need for restrictive definitions. Meaning arises from the very lack of limitation rather than from the logician's narrow propositions.

"There is the possibility here of the kind of deep meaning that in the present day is commonly encountered only in poetry, music, and painting. Certain concepts seem unapproachable in any other way."

As Pisces spoke, Aquarius felt his attitude gradually change from one of anxiety to a sense of the larger order he had felt in a recent moment of discovery.

Aquarius then continued, "What you say reminds me of the feelings I first had when I was trying to 'hear' the internal sound of the Hebrew word for God, Jehovah or IHOAH (יהוה: Yod/Heh/Vav/Heh).* At one point I found an unexpected correspondence with the Egyptian god word IA-AW (𓇋 𓄿 𓄿 𓅱). Something in the flow of the sounds that connect the glyphs convinced me that in each of the languages the names have arisen from the same source.

"My experiences made it seem almost possible for me to share in the understanding of peoples of ancient times simply through the internal repetition of the sounds. It is strange, because we cannot even be sure how the ancients spoke these words! Yet I know that they must have felt in the sound of these sacred words something of what I felt in trying to approach their meaning—it seemed like a movement or music inside me."

"Yes," replied Pisces. "I am sure that we can and do communicate in this way. Real knowledge certainly does not depend on the simple concepts of learning a new fact. What you have said about the sounds used for sacred words by the Egyptians and Hebrews is true of sounds used by many peoples. It was true of the god words used in ancient Sumer and can still be heard today in god names used by the Inuit of North America. Acquiring deeper knowledge through sound is not based on

---

*Note that Hebrew is written from right to left.

contrived ideas gleaned from early peoples or on the mechanical properties of human speech. It depends more on the sincere efforts of ordinary individuals who seek to relate to the higher levels of perception called 'God.' It seems that at the present time, in so-called scientific explanations, there is little recognition of the need to distinguish what is above from what is below, the higher consciousness from the lower such as morality. Until this is realized it is very difficult for anyone to learn from the great traditions."

"How can I gain a better sense of the breadth of understanding that must be represented in these ancient stories?" asked Aquarius. "The sense of meaning that arises from the names for the gods makes me feel that there must be much more to be understood. What about the meanings of the other ancient words? Could I learn to understand their meaning?"

Pisces thought for a moment and then began. "I believe that the particular words you noticed show quite precisely how both the Egyptians and Hebrews approached sacred language. Studying them may help us see just how one might extend the analysis and appreciation to other words. The Egyptian god word you mentioned, which conveys the meaning of 'the One who is the source of all being,' consists of two parts.* The first part, IA (⌐ 𝕊), conveys the idea of Supreme Being by the joining of two sounds: I (⌐), which literally means 'me,' and A (𝕊; figure 3.2 on page 78), which means 'not me.' At the figurative level for A, the sign corresponds with the Hebrew glyph Aleph, א, which is used to evoke a sense of universality. Their combined meaning in the Egyptian root is best seen in other words. For example, the Egyptian word for brain is 'AIS' (⌐ 𝕊 ⌐), in which the added glyph S (⌐) introduces the meaning of discrimination, or distinction. Thus the word for brain quite literally signifies it as the place in which we can distinguish 'not me' from 'me.' The glyphs in reverse order form the word SIA (⌐ ⌐ 𝕊), which means 'the intelligence of the heart.' Taken

---

*For much of the meaning of the Egyptian hieroglyphs, we are indebted to I. Schwaller de Lubicz and her book *Her-Bak, Egyptian Initiate*.

Figure 3.2. Egyptian hieroglyph AS. British Museum.

together, these different usages suggest that it is possible with patience and silence to work toward both the allegorical and hieroglyphic levels of understanding of a word such as IA.

"In the second part of the word, 'AW' (🦅 🦆), we find the A (🦅) repeated, but now it is reinforced by the vowel sound, W (🦆). This sound conveys a sense of place or perspective. The combination suggests the concept of the place of manifestation of universal being: IA-AW (𓇋 🦅 🦅 🦆). In this way, the word directs attention to the special intelligence in us—an inner sense of presence. Prolonged study and awareness of this presence can lead to the manifestation of the Supreme Being within us as individuals. Clearly the ancients saw this occurring through our ability to distinguish between what is 'me' and 'not me.' The silent breathing of the vowel 'sound' is a particularly important aspect of the spoken word.

"We see something similar in the Hebrew word IHOAH (יהוה) with the repetition of the glyph Heh (ה), which refers directly to a sense of 'being.' Heh is pronounced with a soft exhalation of breath. The repetition of the Heh sound in the Hebrew root (הוה: Heh/Vav/Heh) acts in somewhat the same way as the repetition of A (𓄿) in the Egyptian word IA-AW. In the Hebrew word this is an important combination that further develops the concept of 'being.' The glyph Yod (י), with its sense of the potential for manifestation, has the force of the Egyptian short I sound, which is often left unwritten. The concept of perspective conveyed by Vav (ו) signifies the point that separates nothingness from being. So this simple Hebrew word also seems intended to evoke the idea of 'the place of being' within the individual.

"By seeing all these ways of communicating in both sound and form, we begin to perceive the scope of the truths that are presented in these ancient sacred texts. In much the same way that you glimpsed them in your initial readings, some of the translations support the possibility of sensing the concepts directly through the beauty of their poetic expression. But movement from the literal to the deeper levels of meaning needs the support of further content. The meaning incorporated in the glyphs helps to serve this need.

"What we always seem to forget is that finding meaning in either the form or the sound of any word can take place only if we have prepared ourselves for it. And even then it is very important to remember that the effort of attention has to be jointly directed toward both the words that are being examined and toward us as examiners. Understanding cannot be the responsibility of the texts alone!"

Aquarius heard these explanations with a growing sense of appreciation for the prospects that were opening in front of him. "Yes, I see that these books of Moses can lead to the evocation of profound images. If only I could learn how to read them!"

"We could perhaps learn much that is important for us from the ancient texts," replied Pisces. "But special problems may arise when we are unable to gain access to the original languages. Take, for example, the third book of Moses to which you referred, with its story of 'the fall,' or what is sometimes called 'the temptation in the Garden.' We must respect the understanding of the early translators in relation to their time. But important meanings may have been lost, so to understand what has been said we need to have help from the original texts. Fortunately, they seem to have been most carefully preserved, even if not well understood.

"You referred earlier to the three principles in the story: Adam, Eve, and the snake. We have access to the original three-glyph names used in the Hebrew text, which are Adam, Ashah, and Nahash. In Hebrew the names are spelled as:

Adam: Aleph/Dalet/Mem (אדם)
Ashah: Aleph/Shin/Heh (אשה)
Nahash: Nun/Het/Shin (נחש)

"Each of the individual glyphs stands for concepts or qualities. But even without knowing this we can see that Adam and Ashah share the 'Aleph' quality, and Ashah and Nahash share the 'Shin' quality. Each of these qualities is combined with other glyphs that give the words their whole meaning.

"We can try to approach a more comprehensive understanding by looking at the concepts suggested by the individual glyphs. For example,

Aleph/Dalet/Mem suggest: Universality/Divisibility/Passive movement
Aleph/Shin/Heh suggest: Universality/Active movement/Being
Nun/Het/Shin suggest: Individuality/Relative existence/Active
                         movement

"At best these 'meanings' are only approximate abbreviations for the concepts represented by the glyphs. But if we begin with something like them it is possible to start to understand."

"It appears strange to me," said Aquarius, "that by the glyphs Adam is associated with passive movement, while Ashah is active movement. If Adam is a man and Ashah is a woman, are their traditional roles deliberately reversed in this story?"

"No one translation conveys the full sense of the original," replied

Pisces. "Where the translators have lost contact with the intentions of the original, it is a law of the universe that the direction is also lost, and what appears is manifested in an opposing direction. While some of the translations maintain this intention in other ways, in the original Hebrew the story is explicit about important relationships. But this is so nearly completely lost in our time as to require a new understanding, a kind of shock to our way of seeing, before the intended meanings can be rediscovered.

"In an earlier chapter of these books of Moses it was shown that because Adam, the Universal Man, was created in the image of God, he had within him both active and passive principles. However, in tracing the evolution of Adam from the Universal Man, when he was first created, to the Adam found in chapter 3 of Genesis, the translations have emphasized the literal aspect, which encourages us to see him as a physical being. In this false sense, if Adam is a man, then Ashah, Adam's 'helpmeet,' must be a woman.

"We have to be careful not to let the more recent translators' emphasis on the literal cloud a wider perception. For example, once they were committed to Adam and Eve as man and woman, there was no room left to recognize the aspect of Adam that the original called Aish (Aleph/Yod/Shin: איש). It is a Hebrew word that also means 'man.' Failure to distinguish Aish from Adam causes many problems. For example, in the creation of Ashah the story uses one aspect of the whole Adam, an aspect called Tsalla (Tsade/Lammed/Ayin: צלע). The translators called this the 'rib.' However, when the concept relating to the Tsal glyph צ was introduced much earlier in the story, it actually represented a particular relationship between God and man. It is reminiscent of what the Egyptians called the image, or *sekhem*, and later psychology calls 'the shadow.' By not recognizing this relationship, translators missed some of the special qualities of Tsalla. The translation then failed to allow recognition of the properties of Aish that are, in fact, prime attributes of collective humanity, perhaps essential to the wish for action that characterizes this less general level of being.

"A recognition of Aish and his potential for manifestation, as represented in Yod (י), as well as active movement conveyed by Shin (ש), assists us in understanding the relation between Aish and Ashah in the tasting of the apple. Adam, Aish, and Ashah are three interrelated principles that are important at different levels of being and are not confined to the qualities of the masculine and feminine. Overemphasis on gender qualities limits the usefulness of the story as a guide to the search for a deeper understanding."

"What is the role played by this unperceived Aish in relation to Adam and Ashah?" asked Aquarius. "Is the fact that three forces are involved of importance here?"

Pisces paused for a moment before replying. "The idea is certainly important," he began. "But we should first consider the figure of the serpent, Nahash. You will notice in the meanings of the glyphs that Nahash alludes to the idea of the separate individual, what has been called 'the repose of existence,' perhaps an expression of what in narrower, modern terms is sometimes called our nature and in psychological terms the ego.[2]

"If we look a little deeper we can see that our wish for individuality, represented by Nahash, suggests to Ashah, representing our wish for creative action, that it is better to eat of the fruit *heh-etz* (ה-עץ), which grows on the Tree of Knowledge (figure 3.3), than to feed on the usual nourishment, *etz-heh* (עץ-ה), which is available elsewhere in the Garden. The reversal in the order of the syllables in these Hebrew words gives rise to a particularly important contrast of ideas.

"As we noted earlier, the glyph Heh (ה) means 'being.' The syllable *etz* (עץ) conveys the idea of physical substance or materiality. Thus if 'materiality' is given precedence over 'being,' as in the ordinary fruit etz-heh, ordinary nourishment takes place. Something very different must be true when precedence is given to 'being' as with the fruit heh-etz from the Tree of Knowledge!

"In the original story, Adam had been cautioned to maintain a diet of etz-he if he was not to face death. This new fate has been translated elsewhere as if he was not to 'face unavoidable death'[3] or be 'doomed to die.'[4] By eating of the fruit heh-etz, it is Ashah, together with Aish, who attain the knowledge of the gods, knowledge that is necessary for them if they are to see the void that they are—living their lives in sleep.

"By taking into account some of these aspects of the originals, it is

Figure 3.3. A tree of nourishment, from the tomb of Tuthmosis III, Valley of the Kings, Luxor, Egypt.

possible to see that the story is speaking of forces that are manifested in us in different ways at different levels. At one level these forces may create a tension between such apparent opposites as the need for individuality and the requirement for unity. However, when they are put together as conflicting movements within a single individual, they become elements that need to be balanced within us. Instead of elements opposed to one another, they may become the active and passive forces through which the third force is able to achieve the balance that is a sign of the appearance of a new level of understanding.

"The ancient writers appear to require that the readers recognize the oneness from which new being arises within us. They saw that in human attempts to make a whole from its parts, we miss the third quality or force that raises the parts to the level of possible participation in the whole. The process is a little like trying to reassemble into life an organism that has been dissected, when all one has are dead parts. The story points to the necessity for a third force, perhaps the unifying force that resides only in Adam, who was the original creation in the image of God."

After a brief pause to take stock, Pisces continued. "But the story explores these ideas even further. We need to recognize that special difficulties arise when we wish for a relationship between individual and collective existence. Did Nahash, by leading Ashah to taste of the forbidden knowledge, feel the urge to strive toward a knowledge of unity at one level at the expense of a connection with the source of life at another? Did Ashah forget her wholeness in responding to her creative volition? Did the original story intend to remind us of these different levels of being and to question our perceptions of the conditions for their existence? Like Prometheus's fire stolen from the gods, which when given to humans can both warm and burn, the precious nourishment derived from the forbidden tree can either nourish or poison, depending on the state of the receiver. The fruit heh-etz can thus in one case result in despair at the sight of one's nothingness. This would certainly be the case if one holds to the merely personal. On the other hand, it may give rise to great hope if a sense of awareness of a presence greater than the personal has been allowed to remain alive in us."

As Aquarius pondered this insight, the silence grew to several moments. Then he began, "At the level above my usual individuality, I have a sense of my incompleteness. In some ways it even seems that in seeing what I am not, I am better able to appreciate my possibilities, rather than take for granted that I possess special qualities. Can we actually comprehend the universal without an awareness of this lack in ourselves?"

"I believe that what you say is of utmost importance," said Pisces, "That may be why the Hebrew story speaks of a necessary or unavoidable death. Could the personality of an individual, by itself, be expected to understand its own death as a necessary step for transformation? The story reminds us that the knowledge of the meaning of death, like that of life, is truly god knowledge, which cannot be sustained by ordinary nourishment—at least, not by the isolated aspects of personality."

Aquarius understood that it was beyond his capacity to grasp fully, even as the impression settled. "It is a wonder to me," he said, "that Adam, Ashah, and Nahash could be said to be cursed for this acquisition of knowledge."

"You are right!" exclaimed Pisces. "Again, perceptions are too often clouded by our habit of reducing the unknown to the level of our ordinary living, rather than allowing the glimpse of what is higher to lift us above our usual understanding. What is translated as 'curse,' the word *arour* (Aleph/Resh/Vav/Resh: ארור), is based on the repeated letter Resh (ר), which stands for renewal, so the word conveys the possibility of a return to one's real fate. What has been treated in the translations as a sentence passed by a merciless god on his disobedient creations might better be seen as a statement of their possibility of perceiving their 'incompleteness.' Is it then possible that their proper function could be a better experience of themselves in relation to additional levels of consciousness?

"It must be remembered that IHOAH/AELOHIM proclaims that the desires of Ashah will cling to Aish, not to Adam. Aish represents the capacity for manifestation and action, and he is the one who Ashah, the creative spirit, will take as the 'ruler' in their future joint life. This is a long way from the literal rendering that saw only a dictum that a woman would be condemned to be bound to a man. This need for a union is further emphasized later in the story when the Nahash, the 'snake,' is told that in the world outside the Garden, the children 'will strike at your head, and you shall strike at their heel.' Of course, the separate parts of an individual can only be seen to fight if they remain separate from one another. IHOAH/AELOHIM appears to be instructing Adam, and all his aspects, in the universal law that no evolution is possible without the effort that is required to bring our parts into relationship with one another. As humans, we must suffer the many separate aspects of ourselves that are not pleasant to see. But the seeing itself may be the only means of finding the objectivity that permits a conscious striving for a return toward the unity that is found at the level of the gods.

"If these stories can be interpreted as speaking to us of the burdens and sufferings of a conscious person, it is not so hard to understand why great efforts have been made throughout the ages to preserve and interpret them. Humankind in all ages has searched for the best ways to express the wish to try to live responsibly."

The pair again fell silent. Aquarius searched his experiences for the elusive echoes of the truth that they seemed to have just touched, but that were already becoming faint memories. The conversation had come far from his initial questions. While he felt the challenge to make these things more explicit to himself, there was at the same time a sense that the real world was there to touch him and to be touched by him, as though it were the unfamiliar essence of a new age.

Pisces recognized his effort. "I have tried to share with you something about the ways in which I, in my time, have learned that we might begin to perceive meaning in one small portion of these ancient writings of Moses. These perceptions seem to follow naturally from our efforts at creating self-awareness. You will have to go back to your home and life. That is where you can verify for yourself the lessons in the stories. I see that you already understand that there is much more to be seen, that you have the wish to see it, and that you have begun to understand how to work toward fulfilling that wish. It is most necessary to become familiar with what stands in the way of fresh perceptions."

Aquarius rose, and as he turned to leave, he tripped over a falling star and made a wish.

Final Comments

Perhaps it is always the same: attentively listening in on a conversation in which we are not participants leads to unexpected results. The subjects of main concern to the participants in this discussion may have initially seemed well circumscribed. But as the discussion proceeded, it diverged into new areas that were not foreseen—or at least had not been pointed out in the earlier parts of Genesis. While we will not return to the questions that arose during the conversation, it is certainly appropriate here to make reference to the themes of Genesis and to recognize one theme that is especially important for this chapter. It concerns the difficulty of distinguishing between "reality" and "illusion."

We need to recognize that teachers have been emphasizing the literal meanings of ancient stories because they have no access to the early accounts and have little basis for critiquing or truly understanding them. The ancient accounts are thus treated as just "stories," told as entertainment rather than as learning tools.

The reinterpretations made possible by Pisces in his answers to Aquarius serve a quite different purpose here. In the first place, we hope they might suggest lines of inquiry about this particular myth that would lead well beyond the level of entertainment. We hope to supplement it with additional myths in succeeding chapters. Readers may be interested in pursuing private study in this vein or in sharing observations with other interested parties.

What we have not emphasized, however, is a second concern that a totally mistaken view may have been promulgated largely through the inevitable loss of meaning that has accompanied the wide dissemination of all stories, particularly those that became parts of freely available religious texts. Of course, it helps to be aware that all literature is liable to the forces of dissipation that our society calls "entropy." This includes the physical loss of written material, poor translations from different languages, direct modification by the religious leaders, and so forth. The ancient Egyptians were especially sensitive to this particular problem and went so far as to recognize it as inevitable, as a universal neter of nature. The tendency for our works all to be subject to entropy was recognized as one of the most important of all. It is represented in Egyptian myths and illustrations by the god Seth, brother of Osiris. We shall have more to relate about them and their myths later in this book.

We wish here, however, to draw attention to one aspect of the danger of illusion. This problem arises when the search for word interpretation takes us down unhelpful deviations from our central path. By looking at the myths of Genesis along with the Sumerian and Egyptian creation myths, we explore a body of parallel literature that we believe provides us with a perspective on the succession of civilizations over millennia. The challenges of understanding myths represented in Sumerian cuneiform and Egyptian hieroglyphs persist into the challenges of interpreting the Bible in spite of it being presented to us in our modern day English. It is our impression from an all-too-superficial acquaintance with the writings of d'Olivet, with respect to the Old Testament, that the realization of the problems of communicating through long periods of time and across very different cultures is in keeping with many other areas of investigation.[5] They are of such magnitude that one almost despairs of being able to undertake sufficient study of all of them and to truly make the remarkable results that surface a part of one's own understandings.

It is, of course, the age-old problem of communication that serves to remind us of the duality of all our perceptions—esoteric and exoteric, internal and external, reality and illusory. This external study of myth can help one to find the place within us that is discovered through them. The study of such opposites leads to discoveries that are supported by insights that lift us to an unexpected level of understanding, maybe even an awakening of higher consciousness. We cannot help but comment on the great good fortune that seems to be ours in this age, the beginning of the twenty-first century, when such new discoveries, both external and internal, seem to be more and more frequent. We wish here to draw additional attention to the importance of maintaining the internal quiet patience that is necessary if we are to find ourselves in the sudden presence of new perceptions.

FOUR

GILGAMESH
The Struggle for Life

The *Epic of Gilgamesh* tells of the interactions of humans and gods using a rich imagery that allows for several avenues of interpretation. Segments of this story were first inscribed on Sumerian tablets four thousand years ago. The epic was first written by the Akkadians and it was fully recorded later by the Babylonians in 1200 BCE. It survived in an oral version until the latter half of the nineteenth century CE in the Caucasus. In his book *Meetings with Remarkable Men*, G. I. Gurdjieff says that his father, a storyteller, knew a version very close to the account told in that mountainous region.[1]

The epic myth can be approached in several ways. At the literal level, the adventures of Gilgamesh in his search for the secret of immortality attracts audiences for entertainment purposes, but the characters and their interactions also show a sensitivity that leads to metaphorical inquiry, similar to that invited by the creation story in Genesis. The wealth of detail reinforces the themes of the Genesis story and encourages us to broaden our inquiry to many other aspects of higher consciousness. At each level of interpretation—literal, allegorical, hieroglyphic, and esoteric—these myths express opposing forces that underlie our personal struggles for a sense of coherence.

When contradictory elements appear they invite a possible synthesis, which Jung called *enantiodromia*.[2]

Modern archaeologists have sought traces of an actual Sumerian king who might have been a model for the story, but such excursions into the literal distract from the main value of the story, which lies in its symbolism, not its history. A favorite of modern and ancient audiences alike, the epic invokes a level of detail that is, at first, surprising. Besides revealing something of the wisdom of ancient humans, the epic shows that, in spite of the changed circumstances of civilization, our essential perceptions and concerns about life have changed little, if at all. In recent years there has been a virtual spate of republications and new translations of this epic. For our own study of modern translations we use both Sandars[3] and Mitchell,[4] the latter which we regard as a sensitive and readable translation, available in English and retaining much of the story's rich symbolism. It is the responsibility of the individual reader, however, to look at what is available and make the requisite effort to choose an appropriate translation.

An overriding characteristic of this epic is its depiction of gods, whose psychological and spiritual motivations enable insights into human behavior, that are difficult to perceive solely through personal experience. Our limited ability to understand these representations is less about an ignorance of the Sumerian or Babylonian texts than about our hard-to-recognize prejudices against accepting that the gods depicted in stories from an ancient culture could reflect our modern makeup. Wisdom exists, however, where we learn to perceive it and when we can circumvent our habitual attitudes and behaviors.

To understand the myth of Gilgamesh is to experience how these early conceptions of gods, or principles, embody our own most deeply felt impulses, desires, and goals. Approaching the text with an open mind allows us to reflect on the universal nature of humans and the vast complexities within us.

The Meeting of Gilgamesh and Enkidu, and the Two-sided Nature of Being

Gilgamesh, the hero-king, is repeatedly said to be two-thirds god and one-third human. He is physically a fully grown, powerful, and handsome man; however, as becomes apparent, physical growth does not complete a being. Gilgamesh displays one-sided, imbalanced, impulsive behavior that continually causes trouble for the people of his city. Part god he may be, but this does not guarantee objectivity. Clearly gods were not "sacrosanct" beings to the Mesopotamians. The people of the town of Uruk reached a point where they beseeched the great god Anu to rescue them from this mighty king, who is "shepherd of the city, wise, comely, and resolute," yet "no son is left with his father," and "His lust leaves no virgin to her lover."[5]

To balance Gilgamesh's one-sidedness, the gods send him Enkidu, a hairy man who lives with the animals. Enkidu is the man who, according to Gilgamesh's mother, "is the strong comrade, the one who brings help to his friend in need . . . you will love him as a woman and he will never forsake you."[6] Gilgamesh acknowledged his mother's wisdom and expressed the hope that he would indeed have such a friend and adviser.

The implication here is that one important side of our nature, the side that the epic implies is our "essential" nature and important enough to be called a king, is still fundamentally unruly. We do not generally accept this perception, yet throughout the epic Gilgamesh is shown to represent that vitally important part of us, perhaps through the part created two-thirds god that is visionary and responsible for communicating with the world of the gods. The beings called "gods," however, are not objects looked to for "worship," as is the case with God in Western culture, but are aspects of creativity that are necessary for our world.

Humans long for freedom, and this basic desire is abetted by the impulsive, naive parts of our behavior. Such a simple impulse, however, needs a broader perspective, one that includes a sense of responsibility that modifies the impulse. There would seem to be little doubt that this is what the ancient authors were demonstrating for the benefit of their audiences, along with themes of cosmic unity, love, and justice. For modern people, raising such issues may be one of the best ways to encourage us to examine our assumptions about building and sustaining relationships with other human beings.

It is sobering to consider that we give more attention to our modern aspirations—such as money and reputation—and our short-term problems than to such fundamental matters. Given the continuing popularity of this myth, we must find it refreshing to catch a glimpse of the larger, freer world of consciousness. How else might we find the capacity to judge our own impulsive behaviors, which seem both dangerous and attractive?

The epic goes beyond this, however, to show that this "Gilgamesh" side is itself composed of two parts. One of them corresponds with impulsive aggressiveness, but this is countered by a side that is sensitive to far subtler emotions. This early myth, in fact, provides a remarkable counter to modern simplistic ideas of behaviorism that are still invoked today in neurological analyses. It is our view that the sensitivity displayed by Gilgamesh can only with difficulty be attributed to the sympathetic and parasympathetic nervous systems, the view endorsed by modern neurology. Clearly, this myth goes beyond the mechanisms of neurology and shines a light on less-recognized behaviors, places where humans need further development. It identifies different expressions of a deeply felt need for individuality, which in some cases manifests as a kind of longing. This need for individuality must find a balance with other sides of our nature, which develop under other influences. Gaining such insights into our character leads to an internal freedom, one that we continually seek today within the cacophony of Western culture.

The myth describes additional routes of realization as alternatives that each of us encounters in the process of "growing up." All of them may be related to our aims, but the myth makes it clear that perceiving the direction toward the balance we desire requires discrimination that is itself liable to many distracting influences. We rarely find ourselves in a position to weigh their impact on us with any real sympathy or understanding of our actual social and psychological situations. This knowledge is imparted particularly through the character of Enkidu, which has many ramifications.

The Character of Enkidu

In the Gilgamesh epic, the complementary side of the ordinary, natural state is personified by a being named Enkidu, who was created in the literature of Sumer and later subsumed into the Babylonian culture. In the Old Babylonian Gilgamesh text, the most nearly complete text available to us, Anu is said to have heard the prayers of the people and so addressed his wife, Aruru, the Sumerian Ki, who, together with their son Ea, the Sumerian Enki, had been responsible for the creation of humankind. To her he said, "You made him, O Aruru, now create his equal; let it be as like him as his own reflection, his second self, stormy heart for stormy heart. Let them contend together and leave Uruk in quiet."[7] Thus Aruru, with the assistance of her son, created Enkidu, whose name in Sumerian means "the spirit who goes to earth." This spirit becomes a kind of "alter ego" for the great demigod Gilgamesh.

The introductory pages of the Gilgamesh epic show us a remarkable dramatization of the process through which an equal to Gilgamesh became his "second self."[8] Enkidu is the "wild man" who is tamed by being introduced to the world of the king. However, Enkidu, "the spirit who goes to earth," needs help from certain individuals to recollect his original spiritual nature. Before Enkidu is able to help Gilgamesh cope with the world of humans, he must be reintroduced to the world of the gods.

Enkidu first meets Shamat, one of the temple priestesses of the sacred Ishtar who, in the course of their own personal honoring of the goddess, gave their bodies in sexual congress to any man who desired them. We encountered Ishtar earlier, in her Sumerian incarnation as Inanna, goddess of love, who is also goddess of war. Shamat, her priestess, despite the potential dangers associated with this fearsome wild man, agrees to accompany a trapper in search of Enkidu. This is for the purpose of subduing him by introducing him to a knowledge of human interaction that will enable him to transcend his wild state. The description of her encounter with Enkidu, and the necessary six days and seven nights of virtually continuous sexual intercourse required to complete his transformation, is plainly and simply told in the narrative. At the end of it the exhausted Enkidu finds that the wild animals that had been his only companions until that moment now flee in terror. He is to them a total stranger. Enkidu awakens to a new sense of himself as a man, one who feels the need for a companion.

Shamat gradually leads Enkidu through civilizing influences. First she takes him among local shepherds, where he is exposed to human food and is instructed to thoroughly clean himself and don human clothing. Shamat then leads the well-groomed and attractive wild man to the city of Ur, to the man who, she tells him, is destined to be his companion. In fact, she has already suggested to Enkidu that he is perhaps equal in might to the great Gilgamesh. Thus the story introduces us through Enkidu to the concept of the difference between the "natural," as represented by Enkidu, and the "divine," represented by the demigod Gilgamesh, which are sides that can be found within oneself.

The Foundation of Personality in Gilgamesh and Enkidu

The myth explores an aspect of personality that is not well understood or even acknowledged in modern times. Aruru originally placed Enkidu in the world so that he lived in the wild with the beasts. This early life among animals is clearly an allusion to Enkidu's instinctive foundations, the taming of which were necessary for him to play his destined role as someone who could balance Gilgamesh's impulsiveness. In the present world, we do not believe that we can equally trust the two parts of us that we call the "instinctive" and the "intellectual." Since at least the time of Plato, when rational thinking and clear articulation of those thoughts were given precedence, the intellectual has almost always been assigned preferential treatment, at least as the ideal, in cultured society.

Perhaps a similar kind of prescription is being applied here, with the additional suggestion that taming is a factor of early training. Hence the temple priestess is sought to tame the instinctive part. This prescription is, in fact, repeated three times in the epic's introduction: first by the father, who advises his trapper son to seek out the temple priestess to help with the marauding Enkidu; later by Gilgamesh, who gives the same advice; and finally by the trapper, who explains to the temple priestess what he wants her to do. She understands and without hesitation accompanies him. The myth then points out that when the wild man learned the "woman's art" and murmured love to her, the wild beasts with whom he shared his life rejected him. Remember that the reconciliation of opposites allows us to find an internal unity. In this particular instance the reconciliation is achieved through a sexual encounter with a temple priestess, who as a representative of a goddess offers a means to connect with divinity. The unselfishness of the priestess lends an additional transcendent quality to the encounter. This represents the initial preparation of the ordinary self for an awakening of higher consciousness, which in Enkidu's situation leads to his partnership with the demigod Gilgamesh.

Sexuality is thus explicitly recognized in the myth as a force that needs to be reconciled as a conflicting demand of instinctive, wild impulses toward independence and of intellectual clarity. Such a perception may have been much better appreciated in ancient societies, where the passage of the boy or girl into adolescent manhood or womanhood is marked by initiation ceremonies welcoming and supporting the appearance of sexuality as a vital step in personal growth. Evidence of this concept in modern times still lingers in the meaning we sometimes assign to the word *maturity*. However, while adolescence is grudgingly recognized as signaling the impending struggle toward individuality, in the context of the disciplinary, even violent, problems that plague modern families and schools, it is today more commonly greeted with apprehension. This represents a realistic awareness of the genuine potential for destructive self-assertion and violence that occurs when sexuality overpowers the mind.

Unfortunately, human development requires both self-assertion and a need for reassurances; during adolescence, sexual development enters the mix, further complicating matters. Thus the emerging need to express individuality is often seen as a threat to parental or elder moral authority. The Gilgamesh myth demonstrates that this problem has been known from early times. When Gilgamesh and Enkidu are preparing to leave Uruk and seek out the Cedar Forest to kill its cruel and powerful guardian, Humbaba, Gilgamesh consults the elders for their opinion as to how to meet this monster. The original intention of the elders to protect and guide individuality toward its mature expression becomes lost in their fear that the two inexperienced friends may be unable to exercise adequate control. Loss of control is linked to fear and anxiety about new demands made by unfamiliar developments, and is not confined to adolescence. Reactions and coping mechanisms are influenced by cultural attitudes.

We may gain further understanding of the early part of the myth if we examine more closely the repeated symbol of the temple priestess. Modern views about sexual intercourse often offer only two possibilities: it is either a vehicle of ultimate pleasure or a serious duty for the generation of children. The myth enables us to realize that any such simplistic interpretation is inadequate. The temple priestess serves to offer a different point of view, one that recognizes a finer quality of being within us, a quality that is neither sybaritic nor procreative, but transcends these merely personal impulses. Achieving this transcendent state may require outside help, as is represented by the priestess.

We may require a more than ordinary sensitivity to our own natures if we are to learn to appreciate these perceptions of the ancients. Previously we mentioned a special aspect of the creation of awareness within ourselves that is related to sexuality but not to either of the modern viewpoints listed above. This special aspect occurs in the Babylonian and Egyptian myths of creation, particularly in the arising of the first Egyptian god, Atum. The myth reinforces the need to find a level of awareness that approaches real individuation, not simply a stronger personality.

The Gilgamesh epic shows that Enkidu requires a force that transcends both the instinctive wild impulse toward independence and the equally strong demand for the reassurance of relationship. The story directs our attention to the awareness that arises in the presence of powerful sexual energies. Modern day Western morality that denies the power of attraction shouldn't lead one to dismiss its potential for directing us toward the need for higher consciousness. It is the genius of the myth to point out that the unity of being that Enkidu was helped to find through the temple priestess is what conferred upon him the wisdom necessary to play the appropriate role for Gilgamesh.

The Partnership Continues

Throughout the rest of the epic, Enkidu struggles to live up to all that was predicted for him as a friend, adviser, and protector of Gilgamesh. Enkidu enters the city of Uruk, intent on challenging Gilgamesh because the king has been riding roughshod over the people. And so he posts himself outside the marital chamber of a young newlywed girl who was awaiting the king's arrival, as Gilgamesh intends to satisfy his passion before allowing her to proceed with her wedding night with her new husband. Enkidu challenges the approaching Gilgamesh, preventing his entry to the chamber, and the two huge and powerful men contend in a fierce wrestling match, before Gilgamesh, in his fury, tricks Enkidu, causing him to fall to the ground in front of him. But at this point both men suddenly lose their aggressiveness, and instead of continuing to fight, they embrace one another, leaving the young couple to their marriage. Enkidu then acknowledges that Gilgamesh was indeed superior to himself, and the two become the unique friends that Aruru predicted to Gilgamesh in his dreams.

In some ways it is Enkidu who, perhaps because of his former companionship with the beasts of the field, knows better than Gilgamesh the mysterious part that the gods play in nature, including humans. Later in the story he even reminds Gilgamesh of the need to pay respect to the gods at all levels. Communicating with the gods, however, is a function that Enkidu cannot fulfill. Only Gilgamesh communicates directly with them in their own realm.

But we are getting ahead of ourselves. Together the new partners undertake great adventures. It is Gilgamesh's wish to build a reputation that will guarantee his fame and immortality—at least in the world of humankind.

The myth seems to be describing in Enkidu what might be considered his "individuality," a property that in recent years has often been called "personality." The poetry in myth allows for various interpretations, and our perceptions of Gilgamesh and his alter ego may go well beyond a literal understanding. Myth may help us appreciate that we have no basis for supposing that our intellect or our personality provide access to our truly internal creative natures. Our ability to reason is of vital importance in balancing our impulses, but it isn't responsible for the words we use in our relations with others, and it doesn't control the poetry or the music within us.

In Gilgamesh we recognize an essential part of being linked with powers and sensitivities, what we usually call higher, perhaps even magical, values. The myth shows how these two parts of a man, the "natural" and the "divine," even a man who is two-thirds god, are needed if he is to find a true relationship with his whole nature. In this case the balance is found through the clearly necessary intervention of Enkidu.

Further Illusions
in the Land of the Living

As the myth continues, Enkidu guides and advises the naive Gilgamesh, helping him to realize the power of his impulses in the "land of the living," the home of the immortals.[9] Several situations described in detail depict very ancient examples of basic human nature, especially our collective nature. In one example, the friends prepare to venture into the Cedar Forest to kill the monstrous evil called Humbaba, whom Enlil had appointed as the forest's guardian. The myth goes on to show how Gilgamesh marshaled the energy and enthusiasm of the community to help him and Enkidu find the necessary equipment for their undertaking. The community helps them by taking over the construction of huge weapons and armor that most men could not even lift, let alone manipulate. The community meets to carry out the construction of the weapons that the friends wished for, despite the misgivings of the elders about whether they can successfully undertake such a difficult task.

These elders do not take their responsibilities lightly. They are finally persuaded that the urge for the adventure has its real source in the wishes of Shamash, the great Sumerian and Babylonian god of the sun, not simply in the imaginations of the friends in their search for personal glory. Aruru, the mother of Gilgamesh, also realizes that Gilgamesh is responding to an impulse planted in him by Shamash, and so beseeches the god to personally watch over, bless, and protect both her son and Enkidu, whom she has adopted as a second son. She foresees a need for particular care at night and prays to Shamash that when he is elsewhere he appoints the stars and the moon god Sin to continue the watch. The elders agree that, while Gilgamesh cannot undertake the tasks alone, provided he feels fully protected by his companion Enkidu, who has much better practical knowledge and experience, then they too can add their blessings to this undertaking. They advise Enkidu of their concern and stress that he must truly be the guardian of Gilgamesh until their return from the forest.

True to his word, Shamash does indeed watch their trip of six days to the forest to confront Humbaba. And when the critical moment arrives and the friends are still supporting one another, he shouts to Gilgamesh, who can hear the gods, to act at once and slay the beast (figure 4.1 on page 102) before he has a chance to make himself invulnerable to them. This they respond to, and after several dramatic moments of hesitation and self-doubt they summon their courage and joint abilities and slay the monster. After beheading Humbaba, they take the remains to show to Enlil.

Following this episode we find that Gilgamesh is now confronted by a suddenly passionate Ishtar, the Sumerian Inanna, who insists that he become her husband. In a rarely perceptive mode, Gilgamesh points out her history with previous lovers, all of whom, when they inevitably fell into disfavor, suffered dire fates. Of course, Ishtar is incensed by having her nature pointed out in this fashion and ascends to heaven in a rage, where she demands that Anu give her the Bull of Heaven so that she can destroy the unfeeling Gilgamesh. She wins her suit, and the bull is duly brought to Uruk, where it wreaks the havoc expected of such a powerful force. In the end, however, the cooperation between Gilgamesh and Enkidu is equal to the task set before them. Instead of succumbing to this terrible force, they gain control of its ferocity and finally kill it. This is a resounding defeat for Ishtar, in which she suffers humiliation to her pride, as well as the horror of the death of the Bull of Heaven (figure 4.2 on page 103). While at the human level this outcome gives rest and peace to the human participants in the encounter, it resounds in heaven and helps lead to the death of Enkidu, decreed by Ishtar and Enlil as a needful balancing of the power displayed by the partners.

In the end, however, Gilgamesh's development of his personal will over what we unthinkingly call "nature" makes it clear that Enkidu, in his support of Gilgamesh, could not guarantee the necessary functioning at higher levels. The gods Enlil and Ishtar, for all their own impulsiveness, or even because of it, perceive the self-will and pride

Figure 4.1. Cylinder seals of a crowned Gilgamesh with a sword or dagger and an axe-wielding Enkidu slaying the bearded Humbaba.

Figure 4.2. Gilgamesh and Enkidu killing the Bull of Heaven.

that dominates the friends in their accomplishments. As a result, Ishtar decrees that Enkidu must die, forcing an anguished Gilgamesh to realize the truth of the worldly endeavors he believed led to "immortality." The myth suggests that the path to individuality may be a gauntlet of trials.

As in the Genesis story, the price for this internal awakening may be steep. The death of Enkidu marks a similarity in the meaning of the two tales. For both Gilgamesh and the personifications of Adam in the Genesis story, there is a strong movement of pain associated with their awakening. Enkidu represents a vitally important "second self" who knows about the external world in a way that Gilgamesh does not, and the two develop a relationship through trust and love. If we view Gilgamesh and Enkidu as two parts of a single individual, this self-love, which is closer perhaps to self-respect, enables the two parts to act as one. The early events in the epic repeatedly show the effectiveness of a relationship governed in this way in the ordinary world. In the difficult situations they encounter, the love and trust the partners share enable them to carry out their purposes and achieve success.

The myth clearly points out, however, that success in the adventure of life is a powerfully attractive force for our egos. The joint achievements of the two friends reinforce their joy in accomplishment and perhaps distract them from their original aims. It finally leads them to an ambition to "conquer," which results in the disastrous outcome of their life together. In the events that lead up to the death of Enkidu, the myth raises many questions about what may be missing from such relationships with respect to our real needs.

In the end the cutting of the cedars and the killing of Humbaba accomplished nothing. In pursuing their own ambitious adventures, the partners had not even considered the commitment of Enlil to the powers of the natural world for which he was responsible. They sacrificed to Shamash, who could have pleaded their case to the gods, but only after the event. And so Enlil responded by giving their hard-earned booty away, some to the Queen of Hell. The recounting of the adventure ends with a weak recognition of the strength of Gilgamesh, "conqueror of the dreadful blaze; wild bull who plunders the mountain," accompanied by the wry observation that, "the greater glory is Enki's!"[10] That is, the ambition that led Enkidu and Gilgamesh to such wanton destruction ended with the Queen of Hell, ruler of the dead, as the real winner!

Difficulties of Matching Aspirations with Abilities

The myth is uncompromising in its evaluation of the fruits of self-will and ambition in our lives. These interactions with Enlil and Ishtar expose the consequences of such traits. In their adventures the pride of the two heroes led to excesses of action. Their insensitivity killed the guardian of the mysteries of the Land of the Living. Their pride also destroyed the passions represented by the Bull of Heaven and gave rise to taunts and ridicule. Such emotional forces we underestimate at our peril.

In neglecting their responsibilities to the cosmic dimensions of life and attempting to directly grasp what they perceived as the glories, the heroes turned the glories into their opposites. Forces that at one level are a source of generation and development may at a lower level manifest as a desire for power, which can lead to destruction. The myth makes a clear and strong statement that finding the worth in life requires the resolution of opposites through discrimination, which must be found at a higher level than the level of operation of the heroes themselves.

By involving the gods so inextricably in the misadventures the myth shows that the interaction of opposites occurs at all levels; not only our usual lives, but also our most prized hopes and aspirations. The gods live at a level different from humans, and when Ishtar decrees that one of the two partners must die, it seems not to be a retribution, but an inevitability. Enkidu learns of his fate in a dream. As we saw in Gilgamesh's dream of Enkidu's creation, dreams are often used in this myth to illustrate the mysterious nature of the connection between the very different worlds of gods and humans.

With great suffering for both the heroes, Enkidu, so much a part of Gilgamesh's adventures and ambitions in life, is taken from him. Gilgamesh thereby comes to see that his real wish is not for the great feats he and Enkidu had undertaken, but for another, quite different aspect of existence. Behind his original urge to conquer the unknown, he had failed to see the buried sense of his own incompleteness. In the death of Enkidu, however, he is faced with an intimation of his death, which the creation story in Genesis warns is a necessary part of the knowledge of good and evil.

This new awareness finally leads the weeping Gilgamesh, lamenting the death of his friend, to undertake new, lonely adventures in search of the real meaning of life. "How can I rest, how can I be at peace? Despair is in my heart. What my brother is now, that shall I be when I am dead. Because I am afraid of death I will go as best I can to find Utnapishtim, the Sumerian Ziusudra and the equivalent of the Noah from Genesis, whom they call the Faraway, for he has entered the assembly of the gods."[11] He then departs the city of Uruk and sets out on his quest for one who was once a mortal man like himself, but whom Enlil made immortal and set up in the Mesopotamian paradise to the east in the Garden of the Sun.

Adventures in the remainder of the epic graphically portray the strength of the passions underlying Gilgamesh's new ambition to win immortality for himself. The myth repeatedly shows, however, that his wish is not matched by a sense of discrimination. Time and again, the habits of his lifetime lead him to try to use power where sensitivity and subtlety are needed. Only at the end is there a suggestion that he attains a perspective that enables him to see that wisdom involves the resolution of forces rather than their conquest.

Gilgamesh's new struggles resemble those of Odysseus in the course of his homeward voyage. When Gilgamesh finally enters the Garden of the Gods, even Shamash is distressed at his woeful appearance. He notes that, "No mortal man has gone this way before, nor will, as long as the winds drive over the sea."[12] To Gilgamesh he says, "You will never find the life for which you are searching."[13] But Gilgamesh refuses to be discouraged: "Now that I have toiled and strayed so far over the wilderness, am I to sleep, and let the earth cover my head for ever? Let my eyes see the sun until they are dazzled with looking. Although I am no better than a dead man, still let me see the light of the sun."[14] Physical exertion had always accompanied Gilgamesh's passions, and so despite the warnings and discouragement from the gods, he continues in the only manner he knows.

Siduri, a young woman, maker of wine, whom he encountered early in his new search, summarizes his situation with this question: "If you are that Gilgamesh who seized and killed the Bull of Heaven, who killed the watchman of the cedar forest, who overthrew Humbaba that lived in the forest, and killed the lions in the passes of the mountain, why are your cheeks so starved and why is your face so drawn? Why is despair in your heart and your face like the face of one who has made a long journey? Yes, why is your face burned from heat and cold, and why do you come here wandering over the pastures in search of the wind?"[15]

This description presents a cruel contrast between what the friends had anticipated in adventures intended to "establish[ed] my name stamped on bricks" and the fate they attracted by the intrusion of their blind ambitions into the realms ruled by Enlil and Ishtar.[16] Now Siduri accuses him of the folly of searching for the wind, a power that affects all, but that no one can see! Siduri, too, advises him to give up the search. She reminds him that immortality is only for the gods and that he could rejoice in the many substantial things that life offers. "[F]ill your belly with good things; day and night, night and day, dance and be merry, feast and rejoice . . . for this too is the lot of man."[17] Besides, she points out, to find Utnapishtim he has to cross the ocean containing the Waters of Death, and no one but Shamash does that.

Then, perhaps because she cannot control her admiration for a display of will that takes no notice of personal deprivation and suffering, she admits that down in the woods Gilgamesh might find Urshanabi, the ferryman of Utnapishtim. "With him are the holy things, the things of stone. He is fashioning the serpent prow of the boat."[18]

Great willpower does nothing to clarify Gilgamesh's confusion over the nature of his goal or how to reach it. He immediately seeks out the ferryman, but lacking discrimination, in an impulsive attempt to overpower him, Gilgamesh destroys the holy things. These turn out to be devices that ensure the boat's ability to carry Urshanabi over the sea and prevent the Waters of Death from touching him and his passengers. However, Urshanabi too supports Gilgamesh's determination, and so directs him to cut 120 poles, cover them with bitumen, and secure them with ferrules. The two men then launch the boat and travel in three days a journey of a month and fifteen days, to reach the Waters of Death. There Gilgamesh uses the poles one after another to thrust the boat onward without getting his hands wet! When the poles are used up, he strips and holds up his arms and clothing for mast and sail. He thus makes use of the power of the wind to help him, despite the doubts of Siduri and Shamash.

The Power of Discrimination:
The Story of the Flood

Gilgamesh's great efforts bring him across the Waters of Death to the land of Utnapishtim. Utnapishtim sees in Gilgamesh what Siduri saw in him. However, after an initial hesitation, he says to Gilgamesh, "I will reveal to you a mystery, I will tell you a secret of the gods."[19] Then he tells the adventurer the story of the Flood.

The story as told by Utnapishtim is filled with imagery and symbolism rich enough to intrigue the most ambitious of interpreters. Many aspects of it are familiar from repetitions in later Western religious traditions, and parallels with the biblical accounts are striking. We do not review them here. The device of a story within a story is often used in myths to make special points. Two of these seem particularly relevant to our search for a path toward consciousness.

In the first place, we are told that Enlil decided to cause the Flood. This decision makes him sound a little like his great-grandfather Apsu, who threatened to destroy all of creation in order to preserve the conditions for his own comfort. However, Enlil's decision must be seen differently. It was he who separated the earth from the sky. He is the creative force of the wind that in Genesis is the breath on the waters that creates the new possibilities. His impulsive idea of a flood to cure the world of humankind's cacophony was more an attempt to return to pre-creation conditions than an intention to destroy existence.

Enlil's solo venture raises a question: What elements are needed for creation? Ninurta, the god of canals who has his own obvious interest in the life-giving properties of water, points out that Enlil failed to achieve his purpose because he attempted to cause the Flood completely on his own. As Ninurta puts it, not even Enlil could devise without Ea (Enki).

When the Flood is over and the creatures that Utnapishtim saved on his boat have landed safely, even Ishtar celebrates the event with her presence and her jewels. She invites all the gods except Enlil to attend, because "without reflection he brought the flood; he consigned my people to destruction."[20] Enlil's fury when he learns that a mortal has escaped is mainly due to the frustration of his plans. Thus Ea, instead of destroying Enlil as he destroyed Apsu, finds it necessary only to placate him with a combination of cajolery and persuasion, pointing out that a flood is too terrible a punishment for humans.

It thus appears that in the Flood story we have a purposeful repetition of the idea that real actions at any level require a reconciliation of opposites. The impulsiveness displayed by Gilgamesh bears a remarkable parallel to the impulsiveness of Enlil himself. The fact that Enlil requires the moderating influence of Ea invites us to consider the correspondence between Enkidu and Ea. The intellect and reason that they represent play a role in our ability to perceive higher influences. There is an implication here that in our own search we may discover differences in levels of our being that are related to different understandings represented by head and by heart.

The second aspect of the Flood story that is of particular relevance to our interests concerns Utnapishtim's ability to hear and act on the impending danger of the Flood through Ea's whispers to him in a dream. Ea told Enlil that the escape of humankind from his curse was to be blamed on the fact that Utnapishtim had learned of it in a dream! Ea, "because of his oath" to his own creation, had caused the dream.[21] But neither does Enlil question the success of Utnapishtim's survival. Thus Utnapishtim survived that which he should not have, only with the help of Ea.

We have already learned of Ea's use of words and breath as a kind of magic. Ea whispering in a dream is a metaphor that suggests the wisdom that preserves existence comes from levels on high that are difficult to perceive, a finer order than ordinary existence. Evidently messages from the gods are as difficult to hear and act upon as whispers in a dream. In this dream Ea told Utnapishtim to "tear down your house and build a boat, abandon possessions and look for life, despise worldly goods and save your soul alive."[22]

There seems to be little doubt that the secret Utnapishtim mentioned is his ability to hear and act on these words of wisdom. In recognition of this fact, after the Flood is over, when Ea asks the relenting Enlil to take stock and decide what should be done, Enlil recognizes Utnapishtim, who "was a mortal man," as special.[23] Thus he ordains that Utnapishtim and his wife should be granted immortality and "live in the distance at the mouth of the rivers."[24]

The story of Utnapishtim seems designed to draw attention to the question of what constitutes real individuality and levels of consciousness. Gilgamesh continually attempts to reaffirm his sense of individuality and purpose through his physical prowess, but to no avail. This is maintained in the story of Utnapishtim and the Flood, which makes clear how difficult it is for one to discriminate between one's ordinary day-to-day nature and that which is required for higher consciousness. Utnapishtim's abilities are of the required higher order. His ability to hear the advice of a god constitutes a level of comprehension above what may be considered an individual or ordinary viewpoint. This is a rarely recognized perspective that depends on an entirely new dimension of experience.

Utnapishtim's special powers of discrimination are concordant with what we earlier called a change in the level of being. The irony expressed by the myth is that Utnapishtim's ability represents a taste of the wisdom of the eternal for which Gilgamesh seeks, but is totally unprepared to appreciate. The question that it raises for us concerns the personal responsibility we take for the discernment that prepares us to participate in such wisdom.

The final episodes of the epic show how Gilgamesh continues to fail to see what stands in his way. Utnapishtim offers to help him with his wish for an assembly of the gods to whom he can state his case and persuade to grant him eternal life. To obtain this wish, Utnapishtim advises Gilgamesh that he must remain awake for six days and seven nights.

Evidently even the greatest of men, or demigods, needs to remain aware of the demands of the flesh in which they are grounded. Indeed, the demand of Gilgamesh's body for sleep overcomes his intentions to stay awake, and he falls into slumber almost immediately after Utnapishtim tells him the condition of his request. He is not even aware that he slept until Utnapishtim shows him the evidence! Even his passionate wish for immortality is the wish of only one part of his being.

A final opportunity arises through the intercession of the wife of Utnapishtim, who pities Gilgamesh's weary state and admires his past efforts. She persuades Utnapishtim to reveal another secret—another mystery of the gods. Utnapishtim tells him about a plant that grows under the water: "it has a prickle like a thorn, like a rose; it will wound your hands, but if you succeed in taking it, then your hands will hold that which restores his lost youth to a man."[25]

With his customary superhuman effort, Gilgamesh ties heavy stones to his feet and descends into the deepest channel, where he finds and grasps the plant. After returning to the shore he shows the plant to Urshanabi and dreams of how he will take it back to Uruk and feed it to the old men. When that is done he will finally eat of it himself and have back his lost youth.

Alas, Gilgamesh at the end displays that he is yet part man, susceptible to spells of irresponsibility. On his way home, his attention is caught by a refreshing pool of cool water. He neglects his stewardship of the precious plant of eternal life for only the few moments required for bathing in the pool, but this is enough for the serpent who dwells in those attractive waters to sense its sweetness, rise up, and snatch it away. As the tale relates, "immediately it sloughed its skin and returned to the well," stealing the great treasure (figure 4.3 on page 112).[26] Gilgamesh laments that through his efforts he had "gained nothing; not I, but the beast of the earth has joy of it now."[27]

Figure 4.3. Gilgamesh sleeps while the snake steals the secret flower of eternity. Image courtesy of Neil Dalrymple, www.neildalrymple.com.

An Important Aspect of the Love of the Self

The self-love that psychology and morality alike so often view as a source of selfishness and blindness in our relations with others is certainly an important attribute of personality—one that is not easy to see in oneself. Gilgamesh and Enkidu in their active support of each other often show a kind of self-assured disregard for the sensibilities of other people, and sometimes of gods. The consequences of this are examined later. However, we also need to understand a quite different aspect of self-love that the myth emphasizes—one that is a source of mutual trust and respect between different parts of our natures. In fact, this trust confers on the friends a freedom to undertake their remarkable adventures together.

The myth emphasizes, however, that in the absence of the ability of either of the "partners" to dominate or control the other, their working together depends on the power of attraction that is described as "like the love of a woman."[28] Anu's original commission to Aruru implies that this attraction may depend partly on the fact that Enkidu was created so much in the image of Gilgamesh himself. However, this doesn't explain the way they work together. Here, in this power of attraction, the myth shows that development depends on an aspect of love of the Self that has a very different effect than our usual concept of self-love.

The story makes it clear that the love between the parts of our being that these friends represent results in the trust that instinctively and completely supports the very different aspects of their natures in their many demanding and daring adventures. Enkidu is always the trustworthy moderating influence necessary to balance the unruly, adventurous force that is Gilgamesh. He seems to feel equal to almost any challenge. But without Enkidu, Gilgamesh behaves like an unrestrained child, liable to impulsive, even violent and destructive behavior, at the same time lacking the attentiveness provided by a sense of remembering. By contrast, without Gilgamesh, Enkidu's life lacks direction and a sense of ambition. Neither Gilgamesh nor Enkidu was interested in higher purpose until the gods intervened in their lives.

We can see in Enkidu parallels with Nahash in the Genesis myth. First, both of them represent a wish for a sense of individuality. But in the Gilgamesh myth, through the love they have toward their complementary parts, this wish seems to transcend self-pride or self-assertion. Second, Enkidu and Nahash reflect a concern that their "essential" nature, represented by their partners, Gilgamesh and Adam, should realize its full potential. As a result they act to balance a certain naïveté in the creative impulse to action, which is a necessary step in development. While these actions require participation of the more sensitive, emotional parts, they cannot be undertaken without support from the more substantial, worldly side.

Complementary to the Myth of Gilgamesh as written by the Babylonians in the mid-second millennium BCE, there is recorded on a Sumerian tablet from the third millennium BCE a much earlier story, called *Gilgamesh, Enkidu, and the Netherworld*, that speaks of the conditions necessary to maintain this trust.[29] In this tale Enkidu descends to the underworld to help Gilgamesh recover the (possibly tainted?) gifts given him by Inanna. In his descent, however, Enkidu fails to heed detailed directions and warnings given him by Gilgamesh, who is better informed about this part of the world. As a result, Enkidu dies. Gilgamesh seeks the help of Enlil, who refuses to pay attention to his request. It is then Ea (Enki) who assists Enkidu to re-ascend to his friend. However, by the time this help arrives all that is left of Enkidu is a ghost. The reduction in the power of Enkidu from his descent is a strong reminder of the need for close attention of the two sides for each other. A conscious sense of responsibility for both giving and receiving help is needed. The myth implies that a unity of our sense of being or its capacity for action cannot be sustained by our automatic functioning alone.

The Gilgamesh epic thus portrays an unusual power in a human being—the power to struggle against the forces of nature as well as against the habits formed during life on earth. The hero-king's aspirations often place him in opposition to the gods. However, this is not so much the result of intentional confrontations as of unintentional consequences of his insistent, indiscriminate exploration of the limits of his abilities.

He does not succumb to the advice that he should act like other men and enjoy the many good things of an ordinary life, such as food, drink, and relationships. He listens instead to his own restless inner nature, and with superhuman but short-lived effort pursues his quest to the very limits of possibility. In the end, he seems to understand that his stubborn insistence on exercising his will is the source of his disappointment.

We can sympathize with the seeming inevitability of the results of his efforts. We too have an inkling of our mortality and our lack of awareness. We can even see our wish for individuality, and sometimes can be helped to realize that we can attain individuality only by seeing and recognizing our failures. Gilgamesh's return home to carve his story on stone seems to symbolize his eventual understanding that answers to the questions "Who am I?" and "Why am I here?" are not found in adventures abroad, but through patience and contemplation of the strong but elusive powers within oneself.

Whatever the results of his struggles, his remarkable commitment to them set him apart. The myth says, "He was wise, he saw the mysteries and knew secret things, he brought us a tale of the days before the Flood. He went on a long journey, was weary, worn-out with labor, returning he rested, he engraved on a stone the whole story."[30] Gilgamesh's twisting tale justifies the epithet of the ancients who said, "He was wise!"

FIVE

ANCIENT EGYPTIAN MYTHS OF THE AWAKENING OF HIGHER CONSCIOUSNESS

In the Egyptian Osiris myths, the central figures, Osiris, Isis, Seth, Nephthys, and Horus are all neters—that is they are principles, or gods, that act on higher levels of existence. It is through reaching down from these higher levels to that of humankind that they order and maintain the Egyptian civilization. This approach in the Egyptian myths helps us to explore "god knowledge" and how it relates to the awakening of higher consciousness in the modern-day world—remembering the challenges presented by our sense of superiority that arises from our engineering prowess. As a specific example, by the twentieth century CE it was particularly difficult to understand what is meant by the word *spiritual* as opposed to the *materialistic,* which runs our daily lives. We are only questionably better off now in these early years of the twenty-first century. Is there truly a level of being that is beyond the purely physical existence allowed by science and by that explored in psychology? Is the spiritual not accounted for in expressions of the psyche? The Egyptian myths imply that we must confront this recurring question directly.

The Egyptian myths seem designed to evoke our most subtle levels of awareness and discrimination. Through them we may discover whether we can escape the consequences of the blindness and deafness of preconception demonstrated by Gilgamesh and repeatedly warned of in biblical texts. Loss of attention required for discrimination has been the lot of too many serious seekers of wisdom before us. We require an active attentiveness to both the observed and the observer in us so that we can be awake to the sense of distinction between them. We are not accustomed to dealing with such inner subtleties or to being attentive to a need to discriminate between levels of perception in our usual lives. It is for this reason that we began this book with a reference to the neglected sense of our own "presence." It is not at all included in the way we meet everyday life. Internally we seem to know that only by some effort of development in this direction can we hope to verify that which lurks in inner personal experience and holds the key to our ability to connect two potentially distinct foundations of our being called the "ordinary" and the "spiritual." The Egyptian myth of Osiris may help in this pursuit.

Our Basis for Understanding the Osiris Myth

As with the other myths we discussed previously, the myth of Osiris has a long lineage and was never written down in comprehensive form by its creators (see appendix 1). Although never written down, it was well represented in many carvings, embossings, and paintings. Segments of the myth are widely found written in hieroglyphs associated with the illustrations as well as in stand-alone literature throughout the thousands of years of ancient Egyptian culture. The many texts that refer to the life, suffering, death, and resurrection of Osiris accept the story as universally known, as indeed it must have been to the Egyptians. The material we have in written form was provided by the Greek historian and biographer Plutarch (46–120 CE).[1] Similar to the other myths, we depend on an account written some three to four thousand years after the origin of the legend, appearing in a different language and a different culture than when it was first imagined!

The difficulty of appreciating the meanings of the hieroglyphs (see appendix 2) should not be used to dismiss what has been found in a careful study of Egyptian literature, art, and architecture by R. A. Schwaller de Lubicz.[2] He provides evidence that the Egyptians had a very advanced understanding that led to the construction of the pyramids, assemblages of statuary, and elaborate and beautiful buildings. Their geographical and geometric knowledge was extensive. In particular, he insists that understanding Egyptian symbolism requires differentiation between the logic we customarily resort to in studying and what he describes as "the intelligence of the heart."[3] This is his term for a type of understanding that is related more to our intuitive functions and sensations than to the exercise of logic. This appeal to an aspect of the finer sensations that may arise through contemplation and meditation is very compelling and seems closely linked to alternative medical practices that are becoming better known today through such disciplines as osteopathy.

As a brief introduction to the complexity and subtlety of Egyptian thought, we look to R. A. Schwaller de Lubicz's teachings of sacred geometry.[4] In his book he finds embodied in the Egyptian structures subtle effects on mind and perception that are not well understood today except among a few specialists. Egyptians perfectly understood the basic geometric and geographic relationships among the stars, planets, sun, moon, and earth. Important mathematical relationships were incorporated into the designs of even the very earliest pyramid structures, as well as the much later major temples at Luxor. R. A. Schwaller de Lubicz discovered that long before the Pyramid Texts were written down, the special ratios of π (pi) and ϕ (phi) were built into structures. Such ratios were not understood outside of Egypt until after the time of Pythagoras (570 BCE).

Finally, Egyptian symbolism often occurs in combinations, such as the writing of Egyptian myths on various structures and mummy wrappings with the many figurations and images engraved and painted beside them on the temple and tomb walls. It seems necessary to directly experience some of the modes of presentation they used if we are to approach the meaning of higher consciousness, which the myths were clearly intended to evoke.

Myths of the Mystery of Existence in Ancient Egypt

The myth of Osiris tells of the various stages in the life and relationships of Osiris, who was created by the Great God Atum to become king of the Egyptians. He carried out his duties on earth with the support of the neter Isis. She was born as his sister and became his wife. The Egyptian creation myths tell us that it was through the separation of Nut and Geb that spirit became manifest on earth, and so these two, Osiris and Isis, with their brother and sister, Seth and Nephthys, also considered to be husband and wife, were born and became manifest as children of Nut and Geb. In this way these neters are shown as the primary principles that guide life and spirit on earth.

While the neters Seth and Nephthys do not initially seem to have been assigned particular roles, it is clear from his actions that Seth was a particularly powerful neter, appearing to our earthbound level of perception as a destructive influence. From the higher level of godlike perception, he seems to be the required opposite of Osiris and his creativity. In our modern language we can say that Seth manifested the quality of entropy. That is, he was responsible for dismantling structured manifestations, which we recognize takes place when attention is lacking—lost in the memories of yesterday and the dreams of tomorrow. In keeping with this theme, his sister and wife, Nephthys, is said to have been queen of the part of the sky that is always invisible from north of the equator. This influence is symbolically related to night, darkness, and obscurity, and is therefore an opposite of Isis.

Isis appears in the sky as the brightest star of the heavens, called Sothis by the ancient Egyptians, currently called Sirius, and she was a constant companion of her creative brother, Osiris, who is represented in the sky by the nearby constellation of Orion. These forms of the neters as constellations and stars were recognized in the Pyramid Texts as being involved in the process of akhification. That is, they are engaged in the act of becoming one of the highest beings of the spirit world. Within this metaphysical setting the mystical story of Osiris unfolds. R. A. Schwaller de Lubicz points out that the only way we can understand the concept of wholeness is through our ability to appreciate the effects of a whole being divided into parts.[5] This notion is explored further in appendix 3.

Symbols of Family Relationships

Osiris is referred to as the son of Ra, in the sense that the Ra who descends from his daily existence in the sky into the Duat at night is the father of the "sun" of this unmanifested world. Ra is also the father of Nut, the neter of the sky in which he appears by day, and who by union with the earth neter, Geb, gave birth to the family of gods: Osiris, Isis, Nephthys, and Seth. Thus in his lineage Osiris is also the grandson of Ra. At the same time, Nut, the daughter of Ra and mother of Osiris, is called the Mother of All the Gods and is often called the Mother of Ra. Nut is thus both daughter and mother of one and the same god!

Correspondingly, consider the many faces or aspects of Horus (also known as Heru), who in the Ennead lineage seems clearly to be the son of Osiris and Isis. Horus is also known as Ra-Herakti, god of the morning sun. He is one of the chief forms of the sun as it is at midday, when he has the name Ra-Heru-khuti. Horus observes his own conception between the "dead" but resurrected Osiris and Isis in the famous carving on the walls of the Temple of Osiris at Abydos (see figure 5.1). In this instance, Isis appears as a falcon, a form that is often assumed by Horus in his relations with the sun and with Seth.

Isis had hidden the inert body of Osiris that she had recovered in the mythical Byblos and re-enlivened for Horus's conception. She was then constrained by her great love to collect and "re-member" Osiris, prior to his reappearance as the ruler of the Duat. It is through this act that we see

Figure 5.1. Osiris impregnating Isis.
Temple of Osiris at Abydos, built by Seti I.

the Duat as the land of the "Everlasting." This dark and mysterious world
is contrasted with the world of the "day," where the pharaoh reigns, as one
of ordinary time, hence recognizable as a relatively ephemeral world. The
Egyptians referred to this ephemeral world as "Eternity," quite different
from the night, which is "Everlasting."[6]

Such a complex and detailed mythology cannot be expected from
the kind of simple culture purported by some Eyptologists. It is obvious from the social organization that was necessary to sustain the
building of such remarkable structures as occupy the plains of Lower
Egypt, as well as from the subtleties of placement and design, that
the most ancient Egyptians of the early dynasties lived in a highly
organized and complex culture. In the Sphinx (figure 5.2) and the
pyramids (figure 5.3) we do not have examples of toy castles built by
overgrown children, even if the frustration of understanding evident
in the translations and interpretations of some Egyptologists might

Figure 5.2. The Sphinx. Giza Plateau.

Figure 5.3. The Pyramids of Giza. This view is no longer available because modern high-rise apartments have been built in the foreground.

have made them sound so. Once again it becomes clear that we do ourselves a disservice by trying too hard to fit what we find in Egypt into our ready-made molds. R. A. Schwaller de Lubicz in his book *The Temple of Man* clearly shows this disservice in regard to Egyptian mathematics and geometry that, once seen as having a different intent and underlying structure, can be appreciated as sophisticated and powerful as our own.[7]

All our powers of discrimination seem to be most usefully employed to guard against the loss of our ability to analyze our conclusions or against our tendency to substitute imagination for knowledge. When we fail to see past our own preconceptions, we neglect the possibility of detecting what is new in the truly old. If new meanings result, this alone would suggest that we have come closer to appreciating something of the wisdom of the ancients than could ever be drawn from a logical proof that our "insights" are exactly those intended by the Egyptians!

The Myth of Osiris and Isis

Osiris and his sister Isis, the two firstborn of Nut (the sky) and Geb (the earth), while born neters, become king and queen of Egypt. They are responsible for teaching the people of the lands the arts and practices of farming and cultivating the soil, harvesting and storing grain, and making wine and beer. They introduce a code of laws to guide social development and teach humans to worship the neters. In general, they inspire the rise of Egyptian civilization. When this work is accomplished, Osiris temporarily leaves the kingdom in the care of Isis and sets out to instruct other nations of the world. During this period the civilization they had established is so sound that despite the disruptive efforts of their jealous brother, Seth, the kingdom cannot be upset.

Seth, who personifies in both subtle and blatant ways the powers of degradation and destruction, is persistent, and together with his seventy-two comrades and with Aso, the queen of Ethiopia, he plots to get rid of Osiris. They secretly obtain the exact measurements of Osiris's body and have a beautiful box constructed to these measurements. Then, at a banquet, Seth offers the box to whoever is able to fit it. Of course, after everyone has tried and failed, Osiris is persuaded to get into it. He fits! And the plotters seize the box, slam shut the airtight lid, and after sealing it to ensure his suffocation, carry it to the mouth of the Nile and throw it in. This event takes place on the seventeenth day of the month of Hathor, neter of love and motherhood, a day marked as triply unlucky in the Egyptian calendar. It also takes place in the twenty-eighth year of Osiris, which points to his status as a moon neter—a neter of the night.

This disastrous event is immediately known by Isis, who is absent from Osiris at the time, visiting in the village of Chemmis, near Thebes. This place has ever since been known as Coptos, the City of Mourning. When she learns that he has been suffocated, she cuts off a lock of her hair and dresses in deep mourning. She then sets off in search of the body of her husband and brother, accompanied by Anubis, the jackal-headed neter, who, in keeping with the nature of jackals, has a special affinity with the dead. She eventually learns that it was transported by sea to the shores of Byblos, where a great tamarisk has grown up around it. So magnificent was the tree that the local king had it cut down, and the central trunk, which conceals the dead Osiris in his casket, has been set up as the main pillar of the king's huge new palace.

After a number of dramatic adventures, Isis gains custody of the body and transports it back to Egypt. There she opens the casket, and using the power of her attentive love, arouses the body, flies over the erect phallus in the form of a falcon, and conceives the future king, Horus. She then hides the casket containing Osiris's inert body in a secret place and proceeds to a papyrus swamp, where she hides the infant Horus.

Seth, hunting by the light of the moon, comes upon the casket, which he instantly recognizes. He tears it open, rends the inert body of the king into fourteen pieces (twice the magical number seven!), and flings them along the length of the Nile. Isis soon learns of this additional desecration, and after an intensive search, she finds all the parts except for the phallus, which seems to have been consumed by fish. She thereupon makes a model of it from the clay of the riverbank and enlivens it by magic. She then turns the parts of the body over to Horus, Djehuti (who is better known by the Greek name Thoth and who is equated with the Greek god of wisdom, Hermes), and Anubis, who bind and embalm them into a whole body. Thus is Osiris "re-membered" as an "entire" if inert body, so that he can assume his rightful place as ruler. In this process of resurrection, however, he becomes king of the everlasting night, the Duat, and places his son, Horus, in his stead on the throne of the ephemeral daytime of living beings.

Horus, the Son Who Rules by Day, resolves to avenge the suffering and death of his father, Osiris, but is initially unable to trap Seth in direct battle. However, Ra gathers massive forces to provide opposition to Seth, who is clearly in rebellion against Ra's rule. Horus is commander of some of these forces and becomes a principal participant in the warfare. The battles are full of trickery and bitter personal struggles between Seth and Horus, in which the two contestants take different fierce animal forms, wounding and maiming each other, including the rape of Horus by Seth and the castration of Seth by Horus. One source[8] maintains that this battle continued for seventy-two years of earth time.*

At one point in this celestial struggle, Horus captures Seth, binds him, and turns him over to Isis to guard. She, however, through Seth's clever beguiling, a characteristic shared with Sumerian Humbaba in Gilgamesh's Land of the Living, takes pity and releases him. When Horus hears of this, he grows so enraged that he pursues Isis and cuts off her head. Djehuti, who as neter of wisdom was sort of referee of the whole epic struggle on behalf of the court of the neters, finds this violent action unjustified and replaces Isis's head with that of a cow, which explains the close affinity of representations of Isis and the cow-headed neter Hathor. Hathor also clearly has a double nature. At one point in her story she goes berserk and destroys vast numbers of humankind with so much blood-letting that it horrifies even Ra. This provides a second striking parallel between Egypt and Sumer, this time between Isis-Hathor and Inanna-Ishtar who brought down destruction on Uruk with the Bull of Heaven.[9]

In another battle sequence, Seth plucks out the eye of Horus, which, because Horus is an aspect of the sun, is also the eye of the great god Ra, and flings it to the ground, where it smashes into a million small pieces. Djehuti, who constantly observes the battle, sees this event and takes careful note of where the eye falls, collects all the pieces, makes it whole again, and returns it to Horus. This enables Horus, after the battle, to pop this eye into the mouth of his father, Osiris, thus reinforc-

---

*This is the number of years it takes the earth to cover one second of the complete precession of the equinoxes, of which the Egyptians were well aware.[10]

ing Osiris's nature, despite being inert, as a god who is able to offset the mighty dismembering, or entropic, powers of Seth.

Eventually, Seth exhausts his energies and agrees to abide by the judgment of the other neters that he should leave Horus and Osiris in peace, to rule their respective kingdoms. Osiris, the re-membered and resurrected god, is thereafter constantly attended by Isis (figure 5.4). But the Egyptian imagery does not stop there. The myth points out that she is also constantly attended by her sister, Nephthys, neter of the invisible sky world below the horizon at the southern end of Egypt, where the whole drama takes place. Thus, two attentive guardians are invoked: one the neter of the world visible to us at night as the brightest

Figure 5.4. Osiris accompanied by his two guardians, Isis and Nephthys. Nephthys stands to the left of Isis.

star of the heavens, and a parallel neter, invisible in our visible sky.

It seems clear that this myth illustrates two kinds of perception. Conscious perception lies in the sensitivity demonstrated by Isis, which we discussed in the introduction. This kind of perception assists us to be aware of our internal, or esoteric, nature. Nephthys, the neter of the dark, unseen world that we can scarcely comprehend, is symbolic of unconscious perception. This myth points out that we need to discriminate between two aspects of our perception, both of which Egyptians associated with the resurrected subjects that died in our ephemeral world and appeared before Osiris, Lord of Entirety and Lord of the Duat. Only Osiris, because of his own experiences, can point them, with their complete perception, to a new sense of direction. The example set by Osiris invokes the powers necessary for the passage of new candidates to resurrection: discrimination and courage. He points them toward a resurrection parallel to that which enabled him to overcome the forces of dissipation, or entropy, those insidious influences exuded by Seth.

Many subsidiary symbolic elements are contained in the, at times, virtually obscene though dramatic battle between Horus and Seth. It invited paeans of praise and hope, as well as amusement, in much of the Egyptian literature of the New Kingdom. Individual events are rich with symbolism that could occupy a much longer dissertation than we can undertake here. As might be expected, the story is also recalled in different detail, or at least with different emphasis, in various versions of the Book of Coming Forth by Day. One literal interpretation is that the "dead," who are always given the name Osiris, travel through the Duat, and after due "rituals of judgment," emerge to be subjected to the famous *psychostasia,* or "weighing of the heart" (figure 5.5). If the weight of the heart is equivalent to the weight of the Maat feather, they proceed to the Aaru or "Field of Reeds" representing a heavenly paradise in the presence of Osiris. The "dead" request him to grant the blessings of the neters upon them. They are then able to have continued life even as he did when he became the ruler of the dead. Such literal interpretations, in fact, became the model adopted by nineteenth-century CE

Figure 5.5. The weighing of the heart, Ptolemaic tomb, Deir el-Medinah. On the left-hand side of the scale, Horus's right hand steadies the container of the heart. Seth, on the right, in his left hand steadies the feather of Maat.

Egyptologists, who misinterpreted what they saw in the writings and images and prejudged them to be from a simple, literal funerary culture. This intellectualized interpretation obscured the remarkable psychological and spiritual meanings imbued in the symbols of Isis, Nephthys, and Osiris.

Our primary interest is in those dimensions of the tale that speak directly to the questions of time, death, and creation. However, it is worth reminding ourselves to take heed of the warning of the myth that the casket of preconception, which is made to exact individual measurements, was used by the forces of degradation and entropy to suffocate the great king of Egypt! It is even suggested that if Isis (with her perception) had been present when Seth held his banquet, Osiris would never have stepped into the coffin. Yet the myth shows that it is no simple matter to maintain a strong attentiveness. The person newly entered into the Duat must continually guard and protect him- or herself from the vast potential power of Osiris, which helps in overcoming the opposing spirits that dwell in this other realm.

The Roles of Osiris and Isis

Initially the Egyptians emphasized Osiris as a god of resurrection, a role he shared with Ra in his "rising every day."[11] This attribute is also referred to in chapter 17 of the Book of Coming Forth by Day, in which Osiris as Ra is identified with the *bennu* bird, or phoenix. This view of Osiris makes him comparable to the god of many naturalistic religions that have used the symbolism of the springtime regeneration of plants and animals to mark the rhythms of nature and the cycles of the generations (figure 5.6). In several early dynasty documents, Osiris is shown as a god of the harvest, symbolized by an ear of corn.

However, we must be attentive to the full nature of the symbolism. Do concepts of seasonal regeneration fully explain the tenor of the struggles among the neters? Renewal of a beneficent god-being in the natural course of harvesting, planting, and seed germinating, a seasonal rhythm of life and death, seems too passive an image to associate

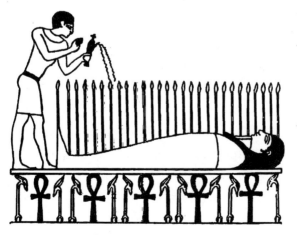

Figure 5.6. Corn grows from the body of Osiris. From Naydler, Temple of the Cosmos, *figure 4.15.*

with the violent events surrounding the death of Osiris, his dismemberment, and Isis and Horus contending with Seth on his behalf. In these Egyptian myths we are dealing with a more extensive and active phenomenon: here we have strong and active positive forces competing with equally strong and active opposing forces. They continually face one another in intense, dramatic struggles.

The Osiris symbols seem deliberately intended to confront our lack of awareness and our passive illusions about what constitutes life. If we remain inattentive we may simply drift through a succession of accidents and minor events between birth and death. This tale shows us that such sleepwalking amounts to a blind and destructive disregard of the vital forces underlying being, which leads to death. In the face of this death, the ability to truly know yesterday and tomorrow needs the power of awakening represented by the immediate and alert attention of both Isis and Nephthys. They represent vital and active conscious and unconscious forces that are required to help us gather our scattered attention, much like Osiris' scattered members, for the real struggle for transformation. Through the union of Osiris and Isis, the re-creation of Horus as king of the present day became possible. But both Isis and Nephthys are needed for the ensuing struggle for the reawakened being.

By such imagery the Egyptian myths parallel the later Christian images of the disciples who slept even in the face of Jesus' impending death. Such images may yet urge us to a more powerful and more personal metaphor for our possibilities. Stories of wisdom are not about others, about the dead, or about events of the past. They are about us, now. The symbolism of the myth of Osiris warns that our part in understanding the difference between death and awakening to life can be played only if we maintain an active role in the continuing struggle between preconception and perception. So rapidly are our fleeting moments of clarity destroyed by our habitual, day-to-day preoccupations that we need help to even be aware of their existence. We need to be fully aware that we are participants in this myth if we are to maintain attentiveness. Only by awakening can we turn toward the possibilities for living as a re-membered being, existing in the everlasting present.

The Egyptian myths, in parallel with that of Gilgamesh, also seriously question our ability to pay attention to our failures, which is required to realize our wish for wholeness. Our appreciation of the Osiris myth depends on the depth of our openness to the human condition. We view our situation with an overly objective intellect, primarily by reference to our analytical memories of past states. But do we not exist outside or beyond such purely mental abstracts or preconceptions? If, for a moment, we attend to our internal aspiration toward wholeness, we see the powerful distractions of thoughts and sensations, nourished by desires and habits formed during a lifetime. However, a moment of actual experience of the fragmentation they generate can help us understand why in the Egyptian imagery of Osiris, his re-membering requires the power of a great god! The forces of distraction, encapsulated in the being of Seth, repeatedly overcome our deepest desire for a sense of unity. Awakening to our actual situation requires great power. Such power will be discussed in chapter 7 when we explore the magic of Heka.

When we become aware of our distracted and fractured condition, it may be possible to taste the remarkable godlike perception symbolized by Isis and Nephthys. Re-membering our entire scattered being requires the special patience, care, determination, and strength that they display. We often experience these characteristics when for a moment we are able to see their absence in us. These myths help us to see that our possibilities depend on a capacity to find and especially to experience the "here" and "now," as opposed to the yesterday and tomorrow of our ordinary level of existence.

Moments of awakening are not ours to command. We are not even accustomed to paying attention to the subtleties of sensation and feeling that exist in us at ordinary times. We scarcely notice either their presence or their absence, unless we are by accident confronted by situations that threaten our lives, give rise to extreme emotional upset, or appear in our dreams. To recall them voluntarily might be possible, but first it is necessary to be aware that we wish to do so. The struggle between the "outside," habitual forces that preoccupy our moment-to-moment existence and the dimly perceived wish for an inner sense of clarity and completeness may be our most serious and important effort toward a better quality of life, but we are oblivious to it. We squander the immeasurable gift of life by our inability to take responsibility for a struggle that could enable us to have at least an awareness of our presence in our life.

The external forces of life are so strong that we take the wish for a struggle against them seriously only when some influence helps us remember that there can be a struggle. This realization of the need for help to mount the struggle is behind the religious teachings of all ages. The wonder that can arise from realizations embodied in the monuments of an ancient culture seems sufficient justification for treating problems the way the Egyptians did—as concerns of the neters. The enlivening of such realizations in our own experience assures us of the existence of the wisdom that we seek.

Only ignorance of ourselves and our situation could lead us to regard these powerful symbols of the search for wholeness as entertaining stories written by a people "of a limited range of sentiment . . . a pleasure-loving people, gay, artistic, and sharp-witted, but lacking in depth of feeling and in idealism," as they were described by Gardiner in the final phrases of his otherwise excellent, if somewhat limited, introduction to *Egyptian Grammar,* first published in 1927.[12] What we seem to neglect in our own efforts is the simple fact that rather than immerse ourselves in anxiety and fear about the loss of our attention, we can always make a new effort to enliven it! This is the message behind these tales of continual struggle and their injunction that the real task of our life is to continually seek the inspiration of the gods to serve the real purpose of both our existence and the existence of those who are in relationship with us.

Osiris in Relation to the Egyptian Experience

Our discussion of the Osiris myth to this point has left out consideration of the attitudes engendered in the Egyptian population by their day-to-day experiences of the seasonal rhythms. They heard these myths repeated each year at the many festivals that marked the seasons of their lives. The yearly rhythms included the Nile's seasonal flooding of almost all the agricultural land. Each year, under the close supervision of administrators and priests, the Egyptians reclaimed the land from the floodwaters. These authorities guided the remarking of the fields and led both the work and the regular celebrations for the common good, which they promoted throughout the year.

The whole population experienced firsthand or knew from family histories the times of plenitude and even more certainly the times of hardship, shortage, and even famine. The unpredictable variations in the seasonal flooding that revitalized and refertilized the fields no doubt had an effect on their lives. The significant uncertainty of outcome must surely have given rise to a sensitivity to their dependence on powers that, while natural, were beyond their understanding. The Egyptian culture attributed the conditions afforded them to the efforts and interactions of the neters. They were responsible for the phenomena of cause and effect in the human world.

We have already noted that the simple agricultural model of the Osirian resurrection relating to the awakening of life in planted seeds seems too passive to associate with the violent, destructive images surrounding Horus's struggles against Seth on behalf of his father, Osiris. However, in the light of the uncertain nature of the yearly flooding, such an association may make more sense. Understanding may come if we study the transformation of Osiris to ruler of the Duat. Perhaps we have misjudged the roles of the neters and their effects on the living. In what follows, we enlarge the scope of appreciation of this central myth.

How the Egyptians could attribute the effectiveness of their own efforts to the attitudes of the neters is difficult to comprehend from a modern standpoint, but we must acknowledge our need for a broader understanding if we are to gain an appropriate perspective. Variations in the natural setting were the background for their experience of the myths, and we must try to place ourselves in a situation of comparable scope in our observations. In particular, we need to try to see what is missing from our conceptions by looking at the many aspects of the myths that relate to the circumstances of Osiris. What in their annual experiences might account for the state, transformation, and eventual fate of Osiris?

Let us consider the seasonal patterns that took place in their land before the dams were built at Aswan. The Egyptians recognized an annual cycle of three principal seasons. Their year began with the river flooding over the land—the season of inundation, or Akhet. This was followed by the season of planting, growth, development, and harvest of the various crops on which they depended for survival—a season of "coming forth," emergence, or Proyet. Finally, at the end of the harvest, the heat of the sun, combined with the dryness, threatened to transform the land to a desert state. These desert conditions were pushed back and held at bay only by the rejuvenating effects of the rising river. The final season of the Egyptian year thus resulted in a period of gradual loss of life-giving powers, or "deficiency," called Shomu. Many unknowns and uncertainties were associated with the season of dryness.

In this setting, the seasonal sequences and their consequences were clearly known to everyone. We need then to turn our attention to the extreme differences that are evident when experienced close at hand, living on the banks of the Nile. To those who depended on the land for their survival, the vicissitudes wrought by the natural world not only would seem to hold their lives for ransom, but might even be considered to be a factor in the eternal struggles of the neters, certainly of Osiris and his sometimes violent and always strong brother, Seth. The myth indicates that the god Horus, son of Osiris, represented on earth by the king, needed to mount supreme efforts to ensure that the forces of entropic decay did not prevail. At stake were the creative forces of magic, justice, and cosmic unity, engendered by Heka and Maat in their support of Isis and Nephthys, who constantly attended to their brother god, Osiris.

Returning to the seasonal imagery, let us view the fate of Osiris as an analogy for the agricultural successions throughout the year. For this it is reasonable to begin with the season of inundation, which is shown as early as the Pyramid Texts to start close to the time of the reappearance of a particular star: Sirius to us, Sothis to the Egyptians, represented by the neters Sopdet or Isis. After the star's seasonal absence, it could be seen again in the sky just before sunrise. This was the time of the new year in Egypt, which marked the recovery of the land at the beginning of the spring flood, a time of enrichment that must have been keenly felt by all.

Teti Pyramid Text Recitation 146 welcomes the event with a tribute to Osiris:

> *Isis and Nephthys have seen you, having found you.*
> *Horus has gathered you,*
> *Horus has had Isis and Nephthys tend you,*
> *and they have given you to Horus,*
> *that he may be content with you.*[13]

The text remarks on Horus reawakening the endangered Osiris at the rising of star Sothis, personifying the neter Sopdet. Up to that point, in the seasonal cycle of Shomu, Osiris existed in the world only as the inert mummiform body. He required their intervention in order to realize his fate. The rising of the river thus appears to mark a reflection on earth of the beginning of a new season in the sky, in which the rising of Sothis signifies Isis finding Osiris's inert body and giving it to Horus. Horus turns his attention to the needs of his father, Osiris, which marks the recurrence on earth of the eternal act of his son, Horus (embodied in the pharaoh), in making things grow on the newly exposed soil.

The inert mummiform figure of Osiris, kept under close protection by Isis and Nephthys, is the actual base from which the harvest grains grow (see figure 5.6 on page 130). In the story we glimpse something of the exchanges between humans and gods. As in the Sumerian creation myths, man is placed on earth to provide essential assistance to the gods; the gods in their turn serve the even higher levels of creative powers represented in the Egyptian myths by the sun, Ra. Yet it is from Ra that humankind is afforded nourishment. This circularity is essential to the continuation of their entire culture.

The rhythms of life celebrated in the annual festivals are of particular importance in understanding the Egyptian view of neters and of humans. These rhythms of life were identified by the Egyptians and recorded in the various versions of the myths. It is also to be found in the basic but important references to the "power of germination" of seeds that exposes the whole process, which offers the hope for the arising of Self and the awakening of higher consciousness.

The Egyptians recognized in the mysterious process of germination two aspects of humankind that they identified as aspects of the body. The first is familiar to us as the physical body. We know it as liable to death and decay. However, the second body, called the *sahu,* is today scarcely recognized by Western culture as a separate entity. The modern biological term for it is *germ plasm,* the conductor of the principal force for biological continuity in all living species. The Egyptians recognized it as the basis for survival of life from one generation to another, that is, as the essential physical basis for a continued influence beyond individual death. In today's modern world, our unfamiliarity with this notion may reflect our loss of perspective about the life process; we have but a vague awareness of something we know as "genetic influence." See appendix 3 for a more detailed exploration of numeric representations of the germinative aspect.

We can further profit by paying closer attention to some of the more abstract references to Osiris, such as his development from the inert state at the end of the creation myths to a more active participant in Egyptian affairs following the end of the battles between Seth and Horus.

We call attention now to the djed column, a hieroglyphic symbol that represents stability. The symbol frequently appears on the walls of temples of the Eighteenth and later dynasties, but was clearly well known for a long time before that. According to some scholars, this column represents the spinal column of Osiris. Figure 5.7 shows Horus erecting the djed column in the Temple of Osiris in Abdos. This temple is one of the finest of those remaining in Egypt, although it is generally less known because it is a few hours' drive north of the principal centers of worship in Luxor. These magnificent, slightly raised carvings in the special Seti I style are located in a room beyond the temple's large introductory chamber. Seti I, in the form of Horus, lifts the column in this depiction.

Figure 5.7 demonstrates the subtlety of the illustrations on temple

Figure 5.7.
The pharaoh Seti I,
as Horus, on the right,
erects the djed column
with the help of Isis
on the left. The small
kneeling figure on the
left is likely another
representation of Seti I
as Osiris. From the
Temple of Osiris in
Abydos.

walls. In this case, the mystery of the Osiris story is not referenced directly, but once we recognize the association of the column with Osiris, we can see how very important such representations are in the story of the continued existence of Osiris, especially the help he requires to play his full, upright role (figure 5.8). In this case we also have an example of the assimilation of the god Horus into the person of the reigning pharaoh. This illuminates a further aspect of Osiris's death at the hands of Seth. Upon Osiris's death, Horus becomes king of the living in his place, while at the same time Osiris is resurrected as the supreme ruler and guardian of the everlasting Duat. Throughout the Osirian legend it is thus repeatedly made clear that the inert Osiris depends on assistance from the living to realize his fate. It is another example of how the

Figure 5.8. Seti I makes offerings to Osiris, the erected djed column. The small kneeling figure on the left is likely another representation of Seti I as Osiris. From the Temple of Osiris in Abydos.

Egyptians recognized the importance of exchange between the worlds to be of utmost importance. This example helps us understand the Egyptian view of the obligatory intertwining of the human world with that of the neters in order that both should fulfill their destinies.

We need, however, to make yet another excursion into how the role of Osiris is entwined with the spiritual development of humans. The use of allegory is an important way that the makers of the myths presented their esoteric knowledge. The neter Min takes a primary role in this example. He is frequently shown on the walls of temples of the Eighteenth and subsequent dynasties as a great neter. Figure 5.9 shows a

Figure 5.9. Min on the left with Sesostris I. From the Temple of Sesostris I on the grounds of the Karnak Temple Complex.

Figure 5.10. The Temple of Sesostris I, reconstructed within the Karnak Temple Complex.

representation of Min from a wall of the small but beautiful Temple of Sesostris I of the Twelfth Dynasty. This temple is now situated among the reconstructions within the Karnak Temple Complex because it was found in pieces within that complex (figure 5.10). Min was also frequently mentioned in the Pyramid Texts and was well known from the earliest dynasties. Although he repeatedly appears as an independent and major neter, it is important to our understanding of Egypt to recognize in him a reflection of Osiris.

Min, or Amun-Min, in which the name Amun means "the hidden one," was also frequently known as Kamutef, which translates literally as "Bull of His Mother." He was almost always shown as an ithyphallic male figure that emphasized his relationship to generation, or more specifically, to the development of what has been germinated (figure 5.11a–b on page 142). It should be noted, however, that Min more

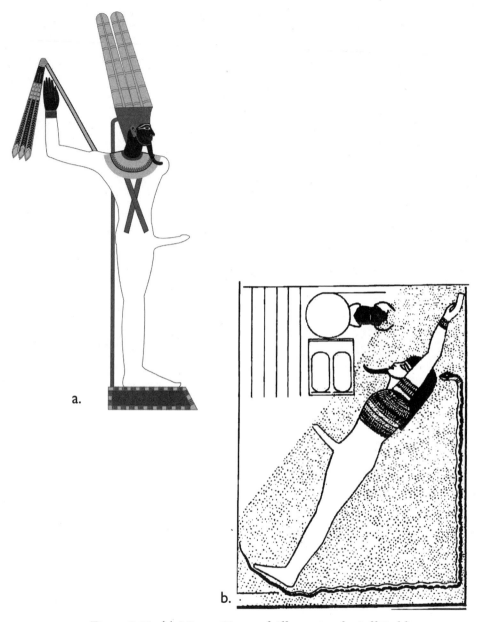

Figure 5.11. (a) Min as Kamutef. Illustration by Jeff Dahl.
(b) Ramses IX as Kamutef.

specifically refers to internal development, or self-development, which we identified earlier as the esoteric aspect of the story of creation. It is thus clear that this figure also represents that aspect of Osiris.

Min seems to represent the culmination of the Osiris myth. That is, the god Osiris, who began as an inert mummy, is represented as an ithyphallic image when seen impregnating the falcon in the Temple of Osiris in Abydos (see figure 5.1 on page 121). He is expressed in our world as an upright and active being in the raising of the djed column, also represented in Abydos (figures 5.7 and 5.8). Finally he is fully represented as Min in the form of an ithyphallic figure (figure 5.9), in which promoting a new creation is his central necessity. It is not, however a "creation" related to sexuality in the sense of external sexual union between a man and a woman, resulting in progeny. Min represents, rather, the generative power, according to R.A. Schwaller de Lubicz.[14]

Min is the son of Isis and Osiris. Later he becomes the consort of Isis. This makes him the father of Horus. This explains the Min-like ithyphallic representation of Osiris in figure 5.1. He is, however, equally often shown as either a close associate of Horus or even identical with him. It's clear we need to remain aware of the many symbols and images used throughout the millennia of Egyptian civilization. These representations served many purposes rather than one fixed concept or idea.

An illustration on the walls of the tomb of Ramses IX offers further information on the importance of the generative function in Ancient Egypt (figure 5.11b).* Here the pharaoh as Min represents the hypotenuse of a sacred right triangle. R. A. Schwaller de Lubicz uses this figure as the basis of his demonstration of the ratios ϕ (phi) and π (pi) that form the basis of the Egyptian representation of generation in mathematics, geometry, and architecture. His interpretations enable us to see that the generative function illustrated by the neters is more related to laws of internal growth, representing the ideals of humankind. The

---

*In his book *The Egyptian Miracle,* R. A. Schwaller de Lubicz derives ϕ and π from the figure in the Ramses IX tomb. He offers a further explanation in *Sacred Science* (184–85), in which he describes the figure as an aspect of the harmonic growth process. In *The Temple of Man* he equates the figure Kamutef with the hypotenuse of the 3-4-5 triangle.

neters do not represent the reproductive function, which is where our preconceptions might lead us.

This illustration has an additional feature that verifies this point of view. R. A. Schwaller de Lubicz was the first to point out that the phallus in this illustration originates from a position just above the middle of the abdomen rather than from the pubic region. In modern anatomical parlance this is the region of the inferior mesenteric plexus, a position that marks the *hara,* an abdominal center of great sensitivity, related neurologically to the solar plexus. This is the position of the "phallus" in all Min representations. This we take as confirmation of the important internal, esoteric significance of this great neter, which links him in function to Osiris.

Min's significance is evident in a major pageant, called the Great Festival of Min, found on the walls of the Twentieth Dynasty temple of Ramses III, called the Medinet Habu, on the West Bank (figure 5.12).

Figure 5.12. Entrance to the Medinet Habu on the West Bank, Luxor.

This temple is one of the best preserved of all the ancient temples of Egypt.

Figures 5.13 and 5.14 on page 146 show one large scene from inside the Medinet Habu. The pharaoh appears seated on his litter, representing the god Osiris. Behind him are two closely standing females, each with a feather on her head, representing Isis and Nephthys. The feathers represent the neters' role as protectresses that are spoken of in chapter 17 of the Book of Coming Forth by Day. He and his entourage are carried in procession behind the figure of Min, who is on an even more massive platform carried by what may be as many as 120 priests (figure 5.14). The ithyphallic Min follows another pharaoh-like figure, representing Horus as Upper and Lower Egypt marching under the winged vulture of Mut, all of whom are led by a powerful bull wearing the crown of Osiris between its horns. This crown on the bull's head is an image of the sun, Ra.

The neter Min had, by this time, the Twentieth Dynasty, become more associated with the son Horus, a god of the living, than with Osiris, who had by now become the king of the Duat. This is supported by the appearance of Horus, who upon Osiris's death became responsible for the fertility and prosperity of the land, shown playing such a predominant role in the procession. While Egypt's spiritual ideas morphed and became tempered over the centuries, festivals in support of the community (and depictions of those festivals) maintained a certain continuity and assurance in the face of those changes.

It thus appears that the image of the inert Osiris, with which the year begins, progressively develops through various depictions, symbolic of the roles he is associated with in human concerns. These developed but less explicit depictions of Osiris allow for a better appreciation of the overwhelming significance of him as the eternal god. While in his major function as king of the Duat he ensures, through his son Horus, the continued well-being of the people of Egypt and of the civilization as a whole.

There can be no remaining doubt concerning Osiris's omnipresence and concerned guardianship of the kingdom of the humans. We thus

Figure 5.13. The left-hand side of the harvest festival procession of Min with the seated Pharaoh, representing Osiris, supported by Isis and Nephthys behind the seat, each with a feather on her head. Mednet Habou, West Bank, Luxor. From Naydler, Temple of the Cosmos, *figure 4.21.*

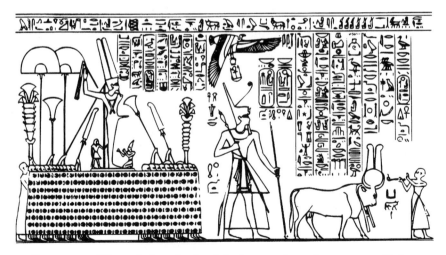

Figure 5.14. The right-hand side of the harvest festival procession of Min, depicting Min on the platform, following Horus under a flying vulture (Mut), led by a bull with the crown of Osiris between its horns. Mednet Habou, West Bank, Luxor. From Naydler, Temple of the Cosmos, *figure 4.22.*

admit to the weakness of our earlier generalization about the agricultural imagery underestimating the power of his story. It does indeed show the Egyptian people's hope for survival through the vicissitudes of life on earth.

A Bald Generalization about the Egyptian Myths of the Mystery of Existence

Throughout this chapter we have examined the myths that represent the story of Osiris. A central concept has emerged from this detailed exploration. A repeated emphasis is placed on the interaction between the worlds of the neters and of the humans as an analogy for our internal Self. This appears in the form of an exchange, which must take place in order for our internal world to continue its existence. This cycle of interaction may thus represent the primary basis for the origin of higher consciousness, which at the same time specifies the usefulness of all our parts: body, soul, and spirit.

These remarkable insights may help explain why Egyptian civilization continued over such a long period, despite phases of fragmentation seemingly related to the invasion of "outsiders." The final throes of ancient Egyptian civilization coincided with the rise of Christianity, followed soon afterward by the appearance of Islam.

The concept of mutuality—a state of reciprocity or sharing, as in the relationship between the Egyptian representation of our internal world as humans and neters—is not well understood in modern Western civilization. As a result, the Western world seems relatively purposeless and in what must surely appear as a serious decline to some; such factors might well lead to a general loss of both personal and collective social values.

The theory of continuous exchange between our various levels of consciousness represented by the two levels of Egyptian existence— the world of the humans and the world of the neters—is dependent on the esoteric aspects of their story of creation and the Osiris myth.

Surprisingly, this understanding must have been intentionally introduced to their society by their mythmakers. Without an open acknowledgement of the esoteric sensitivity of humans to higher influences, represented by the neters, it is difficult to imagine how such a mechanism of cause and effect could have been discovered, or could continue to operate. It is only through one's internal attention to the opportunities afforded by the higher levels of oneself that this whole system can persist.

The essential wisdom expressed in these myths is that the need for wholeness, or oneness, is the most basic, innermost longing of humans as individuals. Without any sensitivity to or awareness of our individual natures, and the consequent superseding of self-interest, we are condemned to a state of disregard and entropy, which leads to an eventual destruction of society. Our present-day lack of perception of this basic need can only lead to disaster. Without the intervention of a higher influence that can fill the place left by our current ignorance of ancient wisdom, it is difficult to see how Western civilization can survive on the basis of technical sophistication alone.

SIX

JOURNEYS THROUGH THE NETHERWORLD

Ancient Egyptian literature implies that certain "prepared" beings are able to experience life on earth in a way that ensures their progress in a desirable direction. For these individuals, entering into the Duat was a natural event in the course of life and was designed to promote the well-being of the spirit. In Egyptian times there were schools for training "prepared" individuals such as the pharaoh and members of his family, his advisers, and his administrators. Teaching initiates to intentionally navigate the challenges of the Duat is the primary purpose of the Book of Coming Forth by Day. Although less is known about the Sumerian culture and traditions, their myths dealing with journeys to the netherworld are consistent with the Egyptian concepts. Separating one's consciousness from the physical body in life (which happens automatically in death) can lead to personal development in the spirit world, which may be the key to the awakening of higher consciousness.

The Egyptian concept that individuals can experience the conditions of the Duat was gradually lost until recently, when new questions about this practice were raised in various ways. Most recently, in the late twentieth century the medical community directed attention to phenomena that have become collectively known as "near death experiences." The results have significantly affected the form and outlook of contemporary palliative care. These experiences have also affected attitudes of a number of current writers toward life and death. Some of them have been influenced by the growing knowledge of what "Western" observers formerly considered "Eastern" philosophies and religions, primarily those from Tibet, China, India, and Japan. But earlier, from the middle of the twentieth century in Europe, extensive studies at both the psychological and mystical levels were referred to by writers such as P. D. Ouspensky, Henri Tracol, and Michel Conge. A number of them discuss the basic teachings of Greek-Russian mystic G. I. Gurdjieff, who worked in France and the eastern United States between 1923 and his death in 1949.

Tracol says that one of Gurdjieff's principal teachings was embodied in the phrase "To awake, to die, to be reborn."[1] This sentiment is said to have arisen in Gurdjieff at least partly through his experiences and studies of Ancient Egypt and his contacts with priests in the Near East, including Anatolia. A phrase reminiscent of it, "Dying before you died," is quoted by Peter Kingsley in his book *Reality,* based on the mystical writings of Parmenides (born circa 515 BCE) and Empedocles (circa 495–435 BCE).[2] Both are known as Phocaeans, a central Mediterranean cultural group that originated in eastern Anatolia and that particularly revered the Greek god Apollo. Kingsley, along with other modern writers whose works appear partly inspired by Sufism, agree that the "rediscovery" of this ancient Greek work concerning incubation gives an impetus to the need felt in more recent times to develop a new sense of what constitutes consciousness, with particular regard for understandings expressed in the thirteenth century CE in the writings of Jelaluddin Balkhi, known as Rumi.

Consciousness is the term for a property that can appear in life, but is difficult to define. Although it is widely recognized and used in relation to living, breathing, thinking humans, it has long been considered as something independent of the physical body and so can continue in some form outside of the body. The authors that we cite above all seem to agree with early Christian understandings that this property is also approachable as a new level of perception during our existing lives, although this requires a form of "preparation," perhaps comparable to what used to be called "initiation." Kingsley identifies it with fifth-century BCE accounts of the word *incubation*. To quote a friend of the authors, "It is not really a question of 'Is there life after death?' so much as 'Is there life after birth?'"

Ancient Egyptian Literature and Traditions Regarding Consciousness

The concept of a consciousness available for cultivation in ourselves appears to have been a central belief of the Egyptians. Their culture, construction, art, and literature strongly support their conviction that consciousness exists beyond our living, breathing, everyday lives. Through a highly structured ritual life, the pharaoh of Egypt was "prepared" by his education. He continually practiced on behalf of the people, as the divine representation of the neters Horus and Osiris. Naydler finds ample evidence for this point of view in the Pyramid Texts of the Old Kingdom.[3] Indeed, current research suggests that they can be interpreted as showing practices similar to what we call shamanism. At all stages of the Egyptian civilization, the role of shaman, or at least of something comparable, is expressed in the apparent participation by the pharaoh in "higher" spiritual powers on behalf of the people. These efforts apparently depended on his special ability, developed during his preparation, to ascend to the highest levels of the spirit world, where he would be able to utilize special "magical" powers. The myths indicate that, as a result, he could heal physical and psychological illnesses on earth, helping disadvantaged souls reach toward the highest spiritual levels.

Whereas Egyptian myths concerning other states of consciousness, as represented in the Late Period (circa 500 BCE), were once dismissed by Egyptologists as meaningless boasting, with improved understanding of Egypt they are now being more seriously examined and studied, even though many remain far from well understood. It is important to note that such mystic states continue to be witnessed and reported as recently as the nineteenth and twentieth centuries and have been studied and evaluated by Mircea Eliade[4] as well as by Paul Brunton.[5]

The Egyptian texts that were first extensively translated in the time of Budge[6] and Sethe in the late nineteenth and early twentieth centuries* were identified as funereal texts. They are certainly texts that address the soul entering the spirit world at different levels of existence, hence Budge's misnaming of the Book of Coming Forth by Day as the Book of the Dead. The information that we have at our disposal about them is not much greater now than it was twenty-five years ago. However, during that time new researchers have observed that these texts also discuss life on earth and have started to reinterpret what they find in them accordingly.

Here we develop more explicitly the concepts of consciousness, rebirth, and the awakening of higher consciousness, as implied in Sumerian and Egyptian myths. Both civilizations exhibit features that direct our attention to the limitations in today's common beliefs and understandings. Based on recent research developments (many presented in publications referenced in this book), it is now possible to identify the beliefs of the soul and spirit developed in ancient times. Both ancient and new publications on esoteric subjects support a strengthening of our perceptions of our experiences, that is, the strengthening of consciousness, or the awakening of higher consciousness.

---

*Pyramid Text numbers were first assigned by Kurt Sethe, who translated them into German and arranged them in a sequence. Allen uses it as part of his concordance of all known Pyramid Texts, compiled in the Ancient Egyptian Pyramid Texts. Throughout this book we use Allen's numbering system to identify the verses by the pyramid in which they are found and a recitation number. Allen gives a full concordance of the verses with the Sethe and Faulkner numbering systems.

Creation Symbols
That Accompany the Creation of Atum

The Heliopolitan version of the Egyptian creation myth summarized in chapter 2 calls for a clearer recognition of our "sense of self." It emphasizes what we refer to as the esoteric aspects of the myth. That is, in the arising of Atum we are called to recognize parallels between what is told in the story and the development of awareness in ourselves, an awareness that allows us to distinguish between the truly animate and the more automatic, even illusory, material aspects of the world. The Egyptian writing contrasts the external physical world and the consciousness within us. This is an important departure in our study of myth. The myths themselves deliberately invoke the arising of this internal sense of self. Recognition of this sense is a critical step in understanding creation myths, one that is necessary to the appreciation of the arising of an animate god in the universe. This is made most discernible in the Heliopolitan creation visions, and is also implied in the teachings of the other major centers of myth development.

We detect something comparable in an important fragment of the Sumerian culture as recorded in the later Babylonian myths:

> *When yet no gods were manifest,*
> *Nor names pronounced, nor destinies decreed,*
> *Then gods were born within them.*[7]

This brief statement calls for us to consider when Anu and Tiamat, the initially existing fresh and salty waters, became mixed in their "turbulent efforts" to unite. This is the image for the first creation of the gods. The phraseology indicates, however, that in parallel with the Egyptian understanding, the Sumerians perceived particular influences, additional to the external concept of creation, that must have been invoked through inner awareness. In the absence of other Sumerian sources, we appeal to Egyptian material for assistance with interpretation.

Although these concepts are not clearly defined in the Egyptian myths either, the Heliopolitan account indicates that something of critical significance is called for if we are to successfully interpret creation mythology. The internal conditions associated with the events attendant on Atum's awakening are key to our understanding the accounts that follow it. In other words, something preceded his sense of awakening, which is critical to the actions and interactions of the neters addressed in the Book of Coming Forth by Day.

The Duat

Through a transition made possible by the combined influence of the neters of magic, cosmic unity, love, and justice, the pharaohs of the late Fifth and Sixth Dynasties were able to enter the world of the spirit and act for the benefit of humankind. We are invited, through the Pyramid Texts, to turn our attention in this direction, toward the Duat, a mystical place beyond our physical world. The Duat, sometimes spelled with a "w" as *Dwat,* exists for the process of the person's higher spiritual bodies of the *ka* and *ba* to join together to form a person's *akh.*

Figure 6.1 shows the Duat, represented as the body of Nut, which forms a passageway through which the sun moves at night. The sun, Ra, is swallowed by Nut at sunset, proceeds through her body at night, and is reborn into our world (below her body) in the morning at a larger size. This complex image includes themes of time, place, and spirit. We are thus able to appreciate some of the difficulties of the early translators of the myths when they tried to describe the place in which our meeting with the spirit world would take place, or to discern what would be encountered there. Our difficulties have only increased because, by the time we picked up the threads of the stories in the nineteenth and twentieth centuries, the clear distinction between esoteric and exoteric that the ancients knew was no longer fully appreciated.

The Duat is quite an "other" world. We refer to it as the nether-

Figure 6.1. The Duat as the body of Nut.
From Naydler, Temple of the Cosmos, *figure 2.13.*

world. Figure 6.1 shows the neter Nut stretched above, swallowing the sun on the left and giving birth to a larger renewed sun on the right. Her body contains stars and shows the passage of the sun through the Duat throughout the night. It does not show a physical earth with a starry heaven above; it represents the world as an esoteric state. This explains why the description of the Duat is so obscure and indefinable.

The physical world does not appear in this figure. Obviously, but also importantly, the Egyptians did not consider the physical world to be the main focus of esoteric creation. What we consider to be the real world of daily life exists parallel to the Duat. The Egyptians viewed individuals as having various levels of being, the higher levels of existence being attracted to the main stream of creation ruled by Osiris in the Duat.

Osiris, who was king in the human world before Horus, showed humankind the elements of "real" civilization. But his jealous brother, Seth, attempted to destroy him through trickery. Seth represents the implacable power of entropy, which destroys all of creation when the magic of perception has been lost. After Osiris's "death" he became king of the Duat. Exoterically, the story of Osiris has been seen as dealing with the spirits of the earthly dead, who must pass through the Duat on their journey of ascent from the human world through the sky to become united with the eternal spirit of light. Esoterically we see the myth dealing with the discrimination within oneself in supporting a path toward our higher consciousness through passage via the Duat. Failing to distinguish between esoteric and exoteric views of the world can certainly lead to confusion. We have presented two difficult-to-distinguish points of view of this world, and even if they are sometimes regarded as virtual psychological opposites, they require reconciliation at a level that is most vital to our understanding.

Naydler's interpretation of the Duat as a world that occupies the same space between the stars and the earth as our manifest world, but is not visible to us except under unusual circumstances, satisfies the conditions symbolically suggested by figure 6.1. The image shows the sun passing through Nut's body at night. Our "daytime" world is below Nut's body, and into it the sun is born with the dawn. Figure 6.1 further shows the sun entering the unmanifest (night) world, the Duat, within the body of the sky, Nut, with our manifest (day) world below her body in the "space" between Nut and Geb, which was created by Shu when he separated the lovers.[8]

Our understanding of the cosmology of Egypt is further enhanced if we trace the replenishment of Ra in his journey through the Duat. Various illustrations in temples and royal tombs of the Eighteenth Dynasty show Shu's role in maintaining the separation of Nut and Geb. In many of these representations of Nut, Shu, and Geb, Ra is shown as a small round sun that enters Nut's mouth as she swallows him at sunset in the western sky. He proceeds through her body during the night and is reborn from her, in the east, at dawn, significantly larger than when swallowed. During the day Ra is carried across the sky by the various ships that conduct the neters on their daily passages. He then returns to the western sky, diminished in size after his daytime work, to be swallowed again at sunset for resuscitation.

Illustrations of the creation process, such as in figure 6.1, often show Shu or Heka supporting Nut's body to reiterate the ancient Egypt belief that they are important spiritual intermediaries. They maintain the air and the space that allow the soul and the spirit to be manifest between earth and sky. The Duat is the place in which the human soul continues its journey of development. Nut, the sky, is a higher spiritual being who was separated during creation from her earthbound lover, Geb, whose spiritual energies, as described in the Pyramid Texts, are directed toward developing the material world. Heka and Shu, who introduced the breath of life into the universe, along with the place where it dwells between heaven and earth, are intermediaries between the earthly material plane and the Duat, where the soul travels to its highest levels represented in the stars in the body of Nut. These same stars are arranged in constellations that reflect the world of the gods. At the higher levels are manifest the mysterious forces that arose with the initial acts of creation of Atum, who represents the arising of the original state of self-awareness.

The figure's depiction of Ra's reentry into Nut during the night suggests a necessary and repeated entry into some aspect of the spiritual world for rejuvenation. In the case of the sun, this act of reentry supports its role of giving sustenance during the day to the human kingdom. But as we will show later the Duat lies within the body of Osiris, where being "within the body" is symbolic of Osiris being ruler of the Duat. The important message for us is that Ra, the sun, is revitalized each night in the same place that the souls of humankind go after death. That is, the Duat is a place where these spiritual bodies receive parallel forms of resuscitation and development in relation to one another on their journey from the human world. This journey of growth takes them toward their ultimate place in the higher world of light, illuminated by Ra.

This explanation helps us understand that the Egyptians regarded creation not only as something that happens to neters at the beginning of the universe or to humans at the occasion of a new birth on earth. Here we are being directed toward an additional and esoteric aspect of creation. It applies likewise to our self-awakening during our lives and to the revitalization and development of souls during their passage through the Duat.

In summary, Ra's involvement in re-creation assists us in understanding the important but subtle dimensions of Egyptian mythology. We are here led toward an appreciation that the sun itself, which by day shines on the earth, imparting life support to all creatures, needs to undergo a renewal during the nighttime. In passing through the body of the sky, Nut, a life energy, whose source is in the light, supplies it with a new vitality, indicated by the larger size of the newborn morning sun. All of this highlights the significance of the Duat, in which this resuscitation takes place. In fact, because the sun passes through the same world that souls pass through at night, we learn something of the process of purification and rejuvenation that the souls go through in the Duat. This process is clearly part of the transformation envisioned by the Egyptians that allows the soul to enter the Duat, the esoteric kingdom of the everlasting ruled by the resurrected god Osiris. Beyond the Duat must reside what we call the "One"—the highest level of consciousness known to us.

It thus appears that the world of the Duat is primarily one in which souls are conferred a new sense of life that enables them to continue their development and passage to the world of the sun. These creative powers must exist in this life, but are not familiar to us, partly because they emanate from and have their source in the higher world of the universal "One." In our materialistic lives we are very far from that.

It is a very different impression from what has been conveyed to most of us by stories about "the afterlife" that developed in other early cultures. In them, it is implied that the afterlife is a place of darkness, great difficulty, and even evil, leading to suffering for spirits; a place to be avoided if at all possible. This does not represent what is found in these tales of the Egyptians.

Reflections on the Nature and Effects of Entropy

We cannot help but speculate that the view of the "afterlife"—as presented in the modern day Western cultures as an evil place designed to make adults expose their past follies and irresponsibilities for which they are held responsible and punished by a god—was likely passed to us by individuals who never experienced the vision needed to allow them to appreciate our individual capacities for development in this world, or the consequences of such development. In the absence of knowledge of Egyptian beliefs, or possibly because of the loss of Egyptian civilization, Western society appears to have substituted moral tales, perhaps believing that humans require discipline from an external force. The Egyptian Duat, in fact, presents complex images of a sophisticated development of consciousness that offers new possibilities, hence new hope, in an existence in which we can scarcely believe because it contrasts so sharply with the pessimistic views to which we have been exposed out of ignorance. Our first responsibility here is to better understand what is said in the Egyptian sources. We may then be in a position to inquire more realistically about the source of our misunderstandings.

We must not, however, jump to any conclusions. We suggest neither that the transition to higher levels of consciousness is simple or easy, nor that it takes place without effort. In fact, the Egyptians indicate that this passage requires a long and serious preparation before tasting higher consciousness as well as afterward. Nor is the passage through the Duat guaranteed to produce any long-term changes in being that might meet our expectations.

What we have noted up to this point is that the Egyptian view of the world that follows a life properly balanced by the feather of Maat does not feature punishment of the human soul. We believe that the Egyptian tradition offers a more realistic esoteric path of hope and of future possibility. This corresponds better with expectations of wholeness or completion, ideals that may be expressed through art, music, or even religious ecstasy, which might parallel in some ways ancient shamanic experiences. Such phenomena may still be recognizable in the great medieval Chartres Cathedral in central France and in the caves of prehistoric people near Bordeaux, France. Such perceptions may also arise during visits to the mysterious remains of prehistoric structures in Mexico, Peru, and Bolivia, or in the highly developed religious structures of Asia, such as in India, China, and Japan.

The signs given in ancient art and architecture, given as encouragement, are so nearly ubiquitous that they must surely command our serious attention. One cannot but ask whether the "modern" neglect of this evidence from the ancient past is not a true illustration of entropy, the degeneration and dissipation of our inner attention, which is a result of our busy human lives in the "ordinary" physical environment.

The Challenges of the Duat

In what follows, we attempt to enlarge on our discussion of the Duat with reference to recent translations of the Egyptian myths. In the next section we will review briefly the rather different but parallel direction suggested by the Sumerian myths, which have also been newly translated.

The travails that are encountered in the Duat seem established to impede or possibly even stop the journey of souls, especially in the case of souls that have not sufficiently prepared themselves for such encounters.* Perhaps it is sufficient to point out that this journey is similar to that of purgatory, a purification state that is taught in some branches of Christianity. Naydler points out that in this journey, after the lower form of soul, the ka, has been set free of the body and has grown accustomed to its strange new circumstances, it joins the ba, and together they can undertake further efforts at purification by overcoming the challenges in the Duat.

The Egyptians taught that three stages are necessary for ultimate

---

*Extensive accounts are presented by Naydler in *Temple of the Cosmos*.

transformation. First, the soul must learn to actively recognize the horrendous images that may come to it in the Duat in the form of strange beasts, perhaps with a dreamlike aspect to the encounter. Some appear as known creatures, such as crocodiles, snakes, wild pigs, or fish, while others are unknown monsters, such as deformed monkeys with horrible faces, threatening rabbits with exaggerated, large teeth, or beasts similar to wild boars, with a vicious intent to attack—images one might encounter in childhood nightmares. These images, seemingly conjured from the imagination, must be objectively recognized in order to stop them. Recognition results in blocking their energies and depriving them of the ability to take "independent" initiative.

The second stage is to enter into a struggle with an opposing force, with the aim of mastering it; there is no intention to kill it. For this the aspiring soul must recognize that this force, perhaps one of the strange beasts, want to steal its heart or eat the magic in its belly. The soul therefore must, at the third stage, turn the threat aside with any diversion that can deflect it from its aim. This act of deflecting the opposing force is sometimes shown in pictures as "the turning of the head" of the threat, which results in the negative energy of the opposition being absorbed by the soul that caused the turning, thus appropriating the energy for its own purposes. For this encounter, the soul is prepared by magical "spells" learned from the Pyramid Texts or the Book of Coming Forth by Day. The following spell appears in the Book of Coming Forth by Day:

> *Get back! Give way!*
> *Get back you crocodile fiend!*
> *You shall not come against me!*
> *For my magic lives in me.*
> *May I not have to speak your name*
> *To the Great God who has allowed you to appear.*[9]

We see that the prepared individual recognizes its opponent, verbally blocks its approach, and offers a threat of its own. In such a way does the ba encounter and dispose of the threats of the beasts and other imaginary objects to be found in the Duat. To exercise the needed objectivity, the Book of Coming Forth by Day teaches that the soul needs to have previously learned the names of the beasts. They can then be recalled, named, faced, and stopped, as though they were real, enabling the soul to continue its passage through the Duat, rather than stagnate within it. This task may even require that the soul gather equipment before death. In the imagery of the Egyptians, besides learning the names of the expected forces, it may be necessary to meet them with the support of an imaginary knife or spear.

The Book of Coming Forth by Day, chapter 31, says:

> As the sky encloses the stars
> and as magic [heka] encloses all that is within its
>   power;
> so does my mouth enclose the magic which is in it.
> My teeth are knives of flint,
> and my back teeth are fangs filled with venom.
> Oh you crocodile who would swallow my magic,
> you shall not take it away!
> No crocodile that lives on magic
> Shall take my magic away![10]

And from chapter 32 of the Book of Coming Forth by Day:

> That which exists is in the hollow of my hand,
> that which does not yet exist is in my belly.
> I am clothed and equipped with your magic, O Ra . . .
> My face is open,
> My heart is upon its seat,
> and the uraeus serpent is with me day by day.
> I am Ra, who through himself protects himself,
> and nothing shall cast me down.[11]

These quotes show just some of the challenges as understood by the Egyptians in having our soul develop beyond our ordinary consciousness. We don't get into the specific concepts of what the "crocodile" images represent, but they can be seen as dream images that we all experience in our lives today. The repeated mention of magic in these verses, and elsewhere in the stories of the Duat, is essential to understanding the meaning of the journey through the netherworld. We deal with the concept of magic more fully later in the next chapter.

With this we complete our brief survey of the properties and possibilities of the Duat. It is an internal world in which a person, starting with an awareness of its Self, prepares to use what help can be found in order to recognize both what it has been and what it might become. Equipped with perception and other tools, the soul begins its passage through the Duat to what dwells beyond it. This further world is the world of light in which an enlivened Ra shines forth as the sun.

This ends our snapshot of the world created by the great god Atum, who through his awareness was able to assemble his own "parts" and give rise to the sense of himself as a living presence in the undifferentiated sea of Nun. In this way the mythology of Egypt seems to point to a wisdom that enables those who can understand it to transcend their ordinary lives and manifest at a higher level of being.

Concepts of the Netherworld in Sumerian Mythology

The Egyptian myths treat the soul that enters the Duat as a new creation, born into a new and different "world," with particular characteristics that enable a new level of being and fresh possibilities. The Duat exists in the space between earth and heaven. This is the same space that Shu opened, and it exists in parallel with our world, yet it is not discernible to us except in certain instances. It can be conceived of as an unmanifested metaphysical world, with links to spiritual ideals. In this sense it is a conceptual world that we seem able to explore through the Egyptian myths. Our question here is whether the same is true of the Sumerian myths.

In approaching this question, we cannot escape facing our limitations in exploring these complex ideas. For some, concepts of life after death come from relatively undeveloped, "fundamentalist" religious views that in Western society were once commonly taught to children. Such views are resurgent in the Western Hemisphere today. Other views of the afterlife result from attempts to make religion more "scientific," as we see in Christian Science, formed shortly after World War I. The scientific outlook has also arisen in other forms since then. Some notions of the afterlife may be closer to motifs touched on by fairy tales or science fiction. They seem to be completely unrelated to the Egyptian perceptions about the nature of the world entered after "death."

The Sumerian myths shed yet another light on the netherworld and provide an alternative view about how and why such beliefs may have arisen. In this section we review a Sumerian story of the world entered beyond life. It contrasts somewhat with the Egyptian Duat. In Sumer, this place is called by translators either the underworld or the netherworld. Aspects of it are revealed in an early myth translated in full by Kramer, which he titles, "Inanna's Descent to the Netherworld."[12] It was retranslated, without a title, in the ETCSL, a translation that enables us to confirm that this netherworld is indeed the same kur that is spoken of in the list of mes, discussed in chapter 2.[13]

In this myth, Inanna, the Sumerian goddess of love and battle, whom the mortal shepherd Dumuzi wooed and won as his wife, decides to descend into the kur. She is a daughter of the moon god, Nanna, and is a sister of the sun god, Utu, as well as a sister of Ereshkigal, the goddess-ruler of the netherworld. In the Sumerian accounts, the sisters, Inanna and Ereshkigal, are said to be bitter enemies, and in keeping with this, there arises in Inanna the jealous and ambitious whim to displace her sister, become mistress of the netherworld in her stead, and possibly to raise the dead! While as adult humans of a modern society we may dismiss such stories as fantastic, they might, if implanted early enough, form part of a fabric of unconscious associations that in our adult life affect our attitudes without enabling us to identify the source, unless it is incidentally presented to us in a myth.

In this story, the goddess Inanna realizes the difficulties of her undertaking and takes elaborate precautions to protect herself. At the beginning of her preparations, in seven cities she abandons what appear to be minor gods. She seeks out and collects the "seven divine decrees" so that she can take them with her.[14] She collects "the crown of the plain," a scepter of lapis-lazuli, an impressive array of jewels and smaller stones of lapis-lazuli, other jewels that sparkle, a gold ring, a breast plate, and all the garments of ladyship.[15] Finally, she puts ointment on her face, and then:

> *My lady abandoned heaven, abandoned earth;*
> *to the netherworld she descended.*[16]

Thus prepared, Inanna walks toward the seven gates of the netherworld accompanied by her faithful attendant, Ninshubur. Before approaching the gates she commands him to return to Sumer, and if, after three days and three nights, she has not returned, to personally raise a loud lament in the assembly halls of the gods. He is to visit in turn each of the three chief cities of Sumer—Nippur, Ur, and Eridu—and with loud and intense lamentations beg the gods whose temples are in each one—Enlil, Nanna, and Enki—to stand by her and "let not thy daughter be put to death in the netherworld," nor let the things that she has with her be ground, broken, chopped up, or otherwise destroyed.[17] She ends her instructions to Ninshubur with the words:

> *Father Enki, the lord of wisdom*
> *Who knows the food of life*
> *Who knows the water of life*
> *He will surely bring me to life.*[18]

Events transpire much as she expects. She arrives at the door of the netherworld, where she acts and speaks "evilly" (which seems to mean that she tries to deceive Neti, the chief gatekeeper, about her real intentions). She demands that he open the doors of the netherworld for her. He does not recognize her, but when she declares herself to be the "queen of heaven, the place where the sun rises," he agrees to consult with his mistress, Ereshkigal.[19] He describes Inanna and her preparations in full detail to his queen and receives instructions to admit her, one gate at a time, and for each gate Inanna must "define its rules."[20] The result is that Inanna is indeed admitted, but at each gate, to her great surprise, she is successively stripped of all her protective accoutrements. When she protests, she is admonished not to question the rites of the netherworld, with the result that when she comes to where she is required to kneel in front of Ereshkigal, she is completely naked. She thus finds herself, without even the symbols of power, humbled before the queen of the underworld, seated upon her throne and accompanied by seven of the Annunaki, who are called "judges." They pronounce judgment upon her and fasten "their eyes, the eyes of death, upon her."[21] She is thus turned into a corpse and hung from a stake. Only Enki takes pity on her plight, wondering why she undertook this adventure. Without the prejudging that we might find appropriate, he assembles the necessary food and water and gives them to two newly created beings, who go to where her corpse is hung. After consulting with Ereshkigal and winning favor by pitying her painful conditions of existence, they are allowed to administer the food and water sixty times to the corpse, thus bringing Inanna back to life.

The rest of the story, including her ascent from the netherworld—which is allowed only on the condition that she replace herself with a soul from the world above—is known mostly from disconnected fragments of a number of clay tablets, some of which belong to other myths. Notable among them are those that discuss the choice of her husband, Dumuzi, the Shepherd King, as her replacement in the netherworld. He does his best to escape, but fate will be served, and after a number of almost effective getaways, he and his devoted sister are required to equally share annual sojourns in the land of death. This sharing of responsibility may be a reference to the relation of Dumuzi and his sister to the cycles of harvest and dry seasons in Sumerian agriculture.

Evaluating the Differences between the Sumerian and Egyptian Netherworld

It is evident from even this cursory review that this strange tale from Sumer, written five thousand years ago, reflects or perhaps exaggerates characteristics that in our time we have somehow come to expect of such a mysterious place as the netherworld, or the underworld, or the world of death, or perhaps the now rarely mentioned hell. The consequences for Inanna and her associates, involving bouts with death, strife, suffering, and evil, interspersed with periods of initiative and life, have reached us almost as archetypes of a mystifying, none too kind, and unstable existence that may follow death. Some doubts must remain as to whether Western concepts are really inherited from the Sumerian or the later Babylonian views of the world after death. They are remarkably similar to views promulgated in much more recent European literature, such as Dante's *Inferno*.

The Sumerian tale recounted above presents a slightly different picture of the underworld than that of the Egyptian Duat. While we need to recognize that we have left out of the comparison the difficulties that may be encountered by new candidates in the Duat, we also see in the Egyptian myths that antidotes are provided for prepared candidates, for which we cannot find parallels in Western religious history. Thus even at the outset of this comparison we must recognize that there are significant similarities between the Sumerian netherworld and views to which we have been subjected as children. We therefore need to clarify the overall significance of both Sumerian and Egyptian mythology to our own time.

While the tales recounted by the Sumerians seem initially very different from those of Egypt, there are significant similarities of detail. For example, while the myths of Sumer speak of the individual participants as though they are men and women, all are actually gods, as are the participants in the Egyptian myths. Like the Egyptian myths, the myths of Sumer are concerned with humankind only as a collection of people, rarely as individuals, at least until after their death.

It thus becomes important to the comparison to recall impressions we have formed from the portrayals of individual gods. It is impossible to escape the sense that the gods of Babylon have the nature of large, long-lived, and powerful but wayward children. These impressions originate from characteristics of the corresponding Sumerian gods, although in this story about Inanna's descent, some of what is told about them seems to border on parody or humor. The exception is Enki (the Babylonian Ea). Aside from him, even the greatest of the Sumerian gods frequently exhibit erratic or unpredictable, childlike behavior that causes them to give in to impulse rather than to objectively assess situations to avoid difficulties. It is as though all the myth writers of Mesopotamia regarded the gods as unconsciously motivated to display extreme behaviors. Gods can't expect to entirely escape fate or to control the inevitable or unknown, but in the Sumerian and Babylonian mythos, they show the opposite of what we have come to view as godlike behavior.

This impulsive lack of control comes as a shock if we expect gods to demonstrate the best attitudes and behaviors. In Egypt we are presented with gods that for the most part correspond to these highest principles of being, rather than fallible persons (except for the god Seth, whom we have identified as entropy, and those associated with him in his counterproductive activities). The Sumerian gods might then be expected to exhibit similar higher levels of being, rather than the base self-aggrandizement displayed in particular by the major goddess Inanna.

Stories from the latter part of Egypt's New Kingdom seem to deliberately go beyond the serious into the realm of humor. Some of them may have been told as entertainment but contained hidden meanings. It is not clear the extent to which the Sumerian tale we just reviewed is a product of similar entertainment mixed with hidden meaning.

Faced with such contradictions to our expectations, it is necessary to question our own naïveté. In this Sumerian account, Inanna's extreme behavior reflects a primitive "reality." But do not our ideas and our ideals about ourselves and our objectives generally contrast with the evidence of "man's inhumanity to man," animals, and nature alike? How do we justify avarice, continual wars, and the destruction of the habitat of beasts and humankind, which we freely admit underlie the whole Western economic system?

The characters of the gods of Sumer highlight the difference between our ideals, of what we routinely believe we are, and the deficiencies, as seen in our day-to-day behavior. Is this presentation of a dichotomy between our ideals and our behavior an admission of faults? Or is this myth a recognition of the outcome of the misfortunes that accompany our infinite capacity to justify our own existence and our habits? These myths were told time and time again in public celebrations and were truly familiar to their audiences. They must have been aware of the subtleties and were able to differentiate between reality and parody. How are we, so removed from the first presentations of these myths, to exercise an appropriate sense of nuance that can sufficiently probe the intentions of the mythmakers?

It must be remembered that the displacement of the Sumerians by Akkadian tribes led to battle, struggle, and suffering. Thus, while we are serious about our wish to perceive in these myths the finer qualities to which thoughtful people can subscribe, we are forced to recognize the influences of war, conquest, and subjugation. The myths seem to represent what might be characterized as family feuding, not the overriding devastation that must have been wrought by armies of the invading societies. The final struggles of Sumer continued for centuries, eventually resulting in replacement of the entire original society by the Akkadians and then the Babylonians. We need to be aware of the many societal changes that took place to adequately understand and compare the stories from the region.

We must also call attention to the turmoil that pervaded Egyptian society between the Old, Middle, and New Kingdoms. There was substantial upset of the political and social situations throughout Egypt that led to struggle, destruction, and upheaval, which strongly contrast with the prosperity and sophisticated culture that appeared in the New Kingdom, eliciting admiration from visitors of other Mediterranean countries, especially Greece. In some accounts the visitors appeared after the flower of civilization had begun to decline, but even in the late periods, Egypt still evinced a higher civilization, one that must have required the religious and mystical support ascribed to the neters Heka and Maat. In other words, we cannot realistically hold to any idea that Egyptian society was less subject to violence than Sumerian society or our own.

We can, however, in the Egyptian myths perceive the remarkable and persistent development of the characteristics of the neters. This capacity for growth and continuity on the part of the mythmakers was not lost during periods of invasion or nonhereditary pharaohs. While Egyptian civilization over the centuries may have experienced setbacks and reversals, from our perspective, across the span of ages, we see the enduring and complex persistence of their world. In the organization of their centralized society into major administrative nomes, or provinces, they clearly maintained a concept of order and responsibility in contrast to Sumerian society, with its battling city-states.

Perhaps the very different social organizations account for the difference in Sumerian and Egyptian views of humans and neters. Equally possible is a basically different initial concept that arose from esoteric elements. Such differences are difficult to pin down by observers from outside the cultures. We can only accept the evidence that we can find.

It is thus important to us to try to place Inanna's expedition into the netherworld in a proper perspective. While struggle and chaos seem to characterize the Sumerian social and religious scenes, we are continually brought back to a remarkable contradiction: the opposing influence exhibited by the great god Enki. He doesn't fit into the superficial mold occupied by the rest of the Sumerian and Babylonian gods. His quiet, considerate, and kind actions are so strikingly different from the strife created by the loud words and louder actions of the other deities that we cannot help seeing the necessity for Enki, who appears as the only possible vehicle for reconciliation of the many conflicting and arbitrary actions of the other gods. We noted in chapter 2 that he was also the principal custodian of the mes.

We are particularly fortunate to have access to this remarkable list of mes. It assures us of the capacity of the Sumerian mythmakers to understand the ramifications of their stories, which we are not easily able to appreciate from this tale of Inanna and others like it. The course of Inanna's descent to the netherworld may be our best evidence for a possibly wider scope of meaning below the surface, which is necessary to appreciate the paradoxes in the behavior of Enki in relation to the the gods. In the story of Inanna's descent, are we not led to see the consequences for humans if we insist, as she does, on finding ultimate salvation in a world of materiality and power?

Only in the light of the whole body of Egyptian and Sumerian myths can we begin to understand the subtlety and precision that is required for their assessment. Such a view displaces our initial impulse to jump to conclusions about the level of perception evident in these ancient myths. Viewing the myths as a whole might even help us recognize elements of wisdom that appear only through a broader perspective. The Egyptian and Sumerian accounts of the development of spirit, and our perceptions of the ordinary levels of externalized mechanical or sleeping individuals, suggest that many lines of approach may need to be used to awaken us to the very different levels of being that are suggested by the pharaohs' journeys through the Duat and Inanna's decent to the netherworld. The two traditions in these earliest myths, taken together, help convince us that they truly understood the full range of perceptions and articulated a clear awareness of higher consciousness.

Egyptian Symbolism of Time

To understand Egypt is to understand the events so dramatically enacted during the rise of Christianity, including the crucifixion and resurrection of the Son of God. Some believe that our daily life, mechanical and uninspired, is truly a death, and that the death of such a life is the only possible beginning of a real life. This is not about the sought-after "life after death" of the literalist-moralist who expects individual reward in a "heaven" peopled by a bearded God and gauzy-winged angels. This is instead a life that recognizes a "necessary death" of much of our unrecognized assumptions about ourselves and about what we say is necessary for the resurrection of being into reality.

In considering our previous explorations it must be evident from the idea that a god can be both mother and daughter or both father and son of another god that we are not dealing with familial relationships or sequences of birth and death that we find within our physical universe. We are not dealing with ordinary ideas of time.

In the hymn to Ra's arising in the Book of Coming Forth by Day, translated by Budge, we read:

> *Homage to thee. . . . Thou risest, thou shineth,*
> *making bright thy Mother Nut [who] doeth homage*
> *to thee with both her hands.*
> *The Land of Manu receiveth thee with content.*[22]

Later, we have:

> *Hail Tatunen, One, creator of mankind and of the*
> *substance of the gods. . . .*
> *Praise Ra, lord of heaven . . . Creator of the gods,*
> *and adore ye him in his beautiful Presence as he riseth*
> *in the "atet" boat.*[23]

In both cases, we expect praise to Ra for his rising in the eastern part of heaven at the beginning of day. In the text this is given as the title of the hymn. But instead, our attention is almost immediately directed to Manu and shortly afterward to the atet boat. Manu is a symbol for the west, and the atet boat is the boat of the setting sun. What kind of "rising" are we talking about?

Evidently, from the very beginning of this hymn of praise, we are invited to a different perspective. We have to realize that the rising of the sun in our day must be the setting of the sun in the day of another. Similarly, the setting of our day is the rising of our night, often a symbol for the Duat and also for the unconscious. These considerations are natural enough in the Book of Coming Forth by Day, and they are interwoven into the relations between Osiris, his son, Horus, and the dead person for whom burial ceremonies are being celebrated. But here, at what is generally considered to be the first part of the text, our concept of time is confronted by this contradiction. This is hardly an accident.

We translate from Budge,[24] chapter 17 of the Book of Coming Forth by Day,

> *Who is this? It is Tmu in his disk,*
> *or (as others say),*
> *it is Ra in his rising in the eastern horizon of heaven.*
> *"I am Yesterday; I know Tomorrow."*
> *Who then is this? Yesterday is Osiris, and Tomorrow is Ra,*
>   *on the day when he shall destroy the enemies of Neb-*
>   *er-tcher [Lord of Entirety], and when he shall establish*
>   *as prince and ruler his son Horus, or (as others say),*
>   *on the day when we commemorate the festival of the*
>   *meeting of the dead Osiris with his father Ra, . . .*
>
> *Who then is this? It is Osiris, or (as others say), Ra is his*
>   *name, even Ra the self-created.*

> "I am the bennu bird [phoenix] which is in Annu, and I
>   am the keeper of the volume of the book of things which
>   are and of things which shall be ."
> Who then is this? It is Osiris, or (as others say), it is his
>   dead body,
> or (as others say), it is his filth. The things which are are
>   and the things which shall be are his dead body; or
>   (as others say), they are eternity and everlastingness.
>   Eternity is the day, and everlastingness is the night.

Here we see that the "day" is defined as the moment of the meeting of yesterday and tomorrow. In this sense Osiris, who is also specifically addressed by his special name, Neb-er-tcher, which literally means "Lord of Entirety," is presented to us as the symbol of the eternal now, that is, the present moment. In other places in the text this is emphasized differently, with Osiris hailed as King of the Everlasting, who exists for millions of years, or Lord of Eternity, thus pointing to two different concepts of the passage of time: the everlasting world and the present eternal moment, which is the now, perhaps the time of the unmanifested world of the Duat.

While it is evident that these texts include an understanding of the fact and significance of death in this world, it is equally apparent that their discussions are not solely limited to the possibilities for the dead person. Rather, attention is specifically directed toward concerns about the nature of time and the manner in which we observe it; we are invited to consider a special concept of living time.

In our world, moments of death are made up of heightened sensitivity for all who are directly associated with them. The Egyptian texts seem to require that we acknowledge the need for such sensitivity for the fruitful contemplation of the situation. This is undoubtedly why modern people consider such texts to be associated with death and burial rituals. In such a state, we are uniquely capable of contemplating philosophical questions: What is yesterday? What is tomorrow? What is the nature of now? What is the meaning of an eternal day that is described in such terms as *millions of years, everlastingness,* and *eternity*? And who, then, is Osiris, who was killed, torn into parts, and reassembled, and then worshipped as the living Lord of Entirety, the equivalent of Ra, great god of the day and the sun?

Can there be any serious doubt that the intent of these passages is to make reference to the glimpses of eternity and wholeness that we are sometimes blessed with in relation to special events of our lives? Such special moments of awareness seem also to be spoken of in the New Testament, at the very beginning of the Gospel of John, in relation to the idea of creation. In this gospel we are given glimpses of the kind of time we call eternity, and reminded that it is associated with the creation of the Word that is made flesh. The same theme seems to be evoked in these Egyptian texts, where we are pointed toward the creation of a wholeness of being in eternity, as opposed to parts of a body in time—living or dead. That is, we are dealing with a sense of ourselves and of existence that is found as a new creation between the death of yesterday and the life of tomorrow, between our memory and our plans.

Those of us who are relatively unaccustomed to dealing with matters of the spirit should take considerable care before denying the possibility that in these remarkable texts the Egyptians, whose entire cultural development seems to have revolved around such concepts, were drawing attention to moments of participation in spiritual matters. We propose here that our most profitable course in pursuing the meaning of the Egyptian myths is to at least tentatively conclude that they were meant to help reawaken our awareness of those barely discernible differences in levels of existence that, while recognizable, and hence available to us, are differences that we forget and neglect in our preoccupation with events or objects in the physical world.

Our day-to-day world makes strong demands on our attention and actions so that we may satisfy the requirements for physical survival. The Egyptian texts make it clear that we must also address another aspect of reality. It is presented as a different aspect of time or existence, one in which what is eternal is not the infinite extension of the "arrow of time"[25] in our ordinary life. In these texts we are being invited to consider a dimension of experience in which the "re-creation" of being that exists for millions of years is taking place within the eternal now.

The Egyptian texts indicate that an experience of this other dimension of time is essential to an understanding of the significance of our existence. However, it is clear, from the references to Osiris as the Lord of Entirety, that even more is involved. To make this explicit, we need to make an excursion into the details of the mystery inherent in the great myth of Osiris as it has come down to us, partly from Plutarch's retelling, but supplemented where possible by what is implied in the myths and hymns involving him. We need to remain very sensitive to our capacity for experiencing our own inner nature, one that we sometimes realize is outside the "normal," which is to say the ordinary, experience of ourselves.

Summary

The Egyptians and Sumerians both show evidence of serious concern with the conscious development of the soul and spirit. In the myths, the material life that takes place on our physical plane was believed to also exhibit characteristics that show the influence of higher levels of consciousness operating within us during our lives. These come from the realms of the soul and spirit. The forces of creation responsible for our world have included within this material world hidden aspects and dimensions of which we are not ordinarily aware. These forces of creation may even enable souls to make use of special properties of preparation, enabling entry into extraordinary dimensions of experience.

The Pyramid Texts and Book of Coming Forth by Day provide accounts and information about the travels and transformations to which the soul could be subject in its development. This information speaks of the capabilities to develop, through experiences in the Duat and beyond it, toward one's ultimate individual purpose. The Egyptians saw this as becoming united with the light- and life-bestowing properties of the eternal sun itself.

In this chapter we have also briefly considered aspects of the quite different styles of presentation: the mystical and poetic approach found in the Egyptian myths compared with the storytelling, prose style of the Sumerian stories. We conclude that both societies understood dimensions of being that go beyond ordinary modern Western concepts. The pursuit of those lost elements in our lives is what led the authors to these explorations.

SEVEN

THE SEARCH FOR WHOLENESS AND HIGHER CONSCIOUSNESS

What is life, what is conscious life, and what do these have to do with the awakening of higher consciousness? Myths provide us with many insights. This final chapter looks in detail at two Egyptian neters, Heka and Maat, representing magic and order, and their roles in supporting a balance of forces within us required to awaken higher consciousness that aims toward a unified whole.

Two Principles of Creation: Heka and Maat

Two major principles of creation occur in the Egyptian myths: Maat and Heka. Maat is a relatively well-known neter, while Heka is almost totally unknown. Without these special beings we cannot understand the full significance of the ancient view of creation and the awakening of higher consciousness. They also provide us with an explicit link to the Duat, enabling us to better understand how the Egyptians regarded appearance in the Duat as rebirth into another world.

Heka is customarily associated with magic, and Maat is linked with cosmic order, truth, and justice. They first appear in the Pyramid Texts

of the Old Kingdom, in relation to Atum after he differentiated himself from his surroundings as a distinct entity. They arise before any
other neters are born, similar to Enki and Ninhursag as described in
the Sumerian fragments of the creation myth. Parentage is not specified
for either one, which implies that they were an essential part of the act
of creation itself. In fact, they are often called "creation gods" by conventional archaeologists. Maat (figure 7.1) has become well recognized
in translations and literary comments concerning the Egyptian view of
life in the later dynasties. She is often mentioned with regard to the
death and the accession of the pharaohs, who were judged on how fully
they respected her properties of cosmic order, truth, and justice. Their
rule of Egyptian society was considered to be "great" when her properties were reflected in their lives and rulings. Because of the frequency of
rituals of invocation of Maat, she may have been the best known of all
of the Egyptian neters. Her role as a creation principle in relation to the
pharaohs is well established.

*Figure 7.1. Maat.
Illustration by
Jeff Dahl.*

Figure 7.2. Heka attending Khnum. Heka appears directly behind the chamber room of Khnum, on the right-hand side, holding the snake's tail. His hieroglyphic name is to the right of his shoulder. From the burial chamber in the tomb of Ramses I on the West Bank, Luxor.

In contrast, her male counterpart, Heka (figure 7.2), seems relatively obscure in the literature outlining Egyptian mythology. He seems to underlie the continuation of creation beyond the first arising of awareness that occurred within Atum. Heka seems to fill a particular need for a strong, active "force" that can support and sustain continuing acts of creativity. That is, while Atum and Kepherer, the neter of "becoming," express the urge to create, this cannot take place automatically or by chance, even among the neters. Heka represents the force of intention that is essential for creation.

Heka's force was needed to initiate the wider scope of creation, a force that emanated from the highest living principle, Atum, and descended in stops and stages into the realm ruled by the pharaohs. This force is so mysterious and unknown to us today that we refer to it as "magic." It is a mystical force that the Egyptians invoked in relation to many aspects of creativity, including the insight that must exist to support the balance necessary for life, even at our mundane level. While our egos might seek to take credit for such insights, on reflection we recognize that its force is really beyond the individual attributes of most of us, belonging more appropriately to the sphere of the spirits.

These two balancing forces, Maat and Heka, underlie and unify various influences essential to the ultimate organization of our world.

A Case for the Importance of Heka

One of the challenges of appreciating the balance between Maat and Heka has been the difficulty in identifying Heka in the texts. He is mentioned by name only twice by Budge in his translation and interpretation of the Book of Coming Forth by Day.[1] In addition, in chapters 23 and 24 of this translation there are several references to "magic" as a noun, which Budge translates as "charms." This clearly relates to Heka's full and proper name as the neter of magic. Heka is also rarely mentioned in the Pyramid Texts. The index to the six Pyramid Texts for which Allen gives translations shows only two dozen references to "magic."[2] Allen's index doesn't mention the neter Heka at all!

Curiously, the name Heka was clearly used in the original Egyptian texts, but in the translations what emerges is an indirect reference to the field of magic. Obviously Egyptologists have been reluctant to closely associate a neter with magic. In our time, at least in the conventional scholarly world, the indirect, less committal reference seems more "objective." We need to keep the reluctance of these scholars in mind when attempting to understand the role of magic in creation, particularly when referring to their translations.

The first mention of Heka (as Hek) by Budge was in reference to a remarkable illustration from the tomb of Seti I that he used in his translation of the Book of Coming Forth by Day. It places Heka clearly in the creation myth of Heliopolis, cementing his importance in the

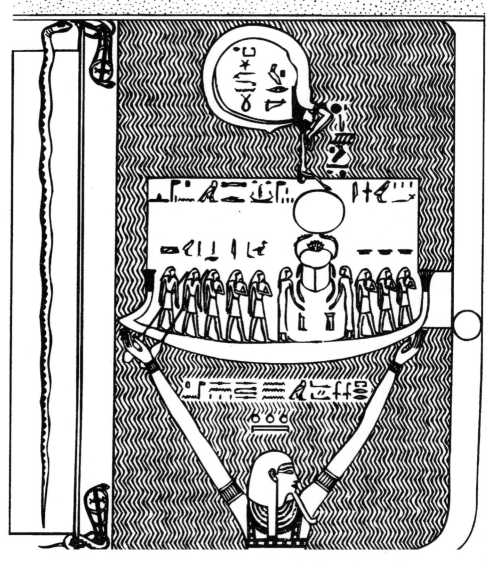

Figure 7.3. Nun, the primeval sea, holds up the boat of creation with Heka and Maat as the third and fourth figures on the left of the scarab beetle. From the tomb of Ramses VI. From Naydler, Temple of the Cosmos, *figure 2.15*.

Egyptian pantheon while offering a more succinct presentation of the created world than is possible with words alone. We present a version of this illustration from the tomb of Ramses VI in figure 7.3.[3]

Figure 7.3 shows an image of Nun arising from the primeval sea, holding the boat of the sun in her upraised arms. In the boat the beetle, Kepherer, holds up the sun disk, which is being received by an upside-down Nut. Although difficult to see, she is standing upside down on the head of Osiris. The accompanying hieroglyphs, in front of Osiris, read "(This) Sky receives Ra." Inside the circle formed by the curved body of Osiris at the top we find written "(This) Osiris encircles (the) Duat." In the boat, Maat and Heka are shown with their early hieroglyphic names above their heads, standing third and fourth to the left of the beetle. Thus, in this one figure we are shown the essential elements leading to the creation of the world of Atum, the world from which Ra eventually arose. Extending beyond this world of Ra is the realm of the Duat, which is here shown to be encircled at the top of the figure by the body of Osiris, who is usually depicted in the Egyptian murals and writings as the neter who rules the Duat. This dramatic depiction shows the main sequence of events that is spelled out at length in the Heliopolitan version of creation.

Figure 7.4 shows Heka and Maat together in an image from the papyrus of Khensumosi. In it, they stand on opposite sides of the great god of creation, shown in the form of Ra-Herakti. They are wearing typical head ornaments of the later dynasties. Heka has the hieroglyph of the hindquarters of a lion above his head, symbolizing the great strength of his special powers. Hanging on his right arm is the symbol for life (the ankh), and below it is the symbol for prosperity or wealth (the *was* scepter). Both of these symbols are also carried by Ra-Herakti. On the other side of Ra-Herakti stands Maat in a posture complementary to that of Heka, with the customary feather of Shu upon her head.

These figures show that Maat and Heka are of great importance in

Figure 7.4. Heka and Maat on either side of Ra-Herakti with their individual insignia: the hindquarters of a lion above the head of Heka, on the left, and the feather of Shu upon the head of Maat. From Naydler, Temple of the Cosmos, figure 6.3.

the Egyptian pantheon of neters. Figure 7.4 portrays them as principles of creation. One more indication of their similarity in importance is that they also appear together elsewhere in depictions for the hours of the day.[4] Maat appears as the first hour and Heka as the tenth hour.

Characteristics of Heka
Relating to the Awakening of Higher Consciousness

As we suggested earlier, the concept of Heka (magic) has been subject to the unrecognized personal biases of the late nineteenth and early twentieth century translators. The Egyptian view of magic is particularly vulnerable to slanted Western attitudes. Christian scholars seem reluctant to accept the neter Heka as a magician, despite the biblical story of the birth of the Christ being heralded by the appearance of three magi, or wise men. Aside from this story, magic and magicians have not been welcomed in the West for several centuries, largely as a carryover from the almost forgotten Inquisition definition of the heretical. Since medieval times, magic has been officially regarded by the Roman Catholic Church as opposed to religion and has often been subject to their official scrutiny. As late as the seventeenth century, near the dawning of the scientific age, Newton was writing somewhat esoteric notes of his personal interests in his diaries in code, apparently so that they could not be easily probed by uninformed readers or inquisitors. In 1662 the Royal Society was founded in Great Britain "to improve Natural Knowledge," i.e., science and rational studies. In spite of this rise in science in the Western world, superstitions surrounding magic continued. For example it was only in 1694 that the last "witches" were burned at the stake in Salem, Massachusetts.[5] The suppression of the concept of witches and magic continued to at least the 1800s and possibly to today.[6] The Inquisition, which lasted for centuries, was clearly not a time for open debates about topics that could be seen as challenges to the power brokers of the day.

We may wonder how such events could still cause unconscious anxiety in today's world. Such attitudes may still live on, perhaps in the form of stories told to us when we were young. The subject is avoided in adult conventional life and seems to have been especially sidestepped in the "serious" scholarly interpretation of Egyptian myths. Indeed, perhaps partly because of difficulties in interpreting the Pyramid Texts, as well as sections of the Book of Coming Forth by Day, mid-twentieth-century translators dubbed the recitations that make up these books "spells," as though they constitute some kind of parlor magic of no real importance. We need to remain fully alert to the fact that this problem can still cause difficulties in modern attempts to appreciate the subtlety of the Egyptian views of creation and of the neters.

As we venture into a more detailed examination of Heka and Maat, it is useful to recall two points we made earlier with respect to the mythology of the ancient world. First, in both the Sumerian and Egyptian myths, as we noted in chapter 2, all of the initial creation took place in the world of the gods. We are therefore considering events in a world whose properties are of a higher, esoteric organizational order than our material world. Second, we need to consider the arising of the neters Ptah and Seth. In chapter 2 we pointed out that the Egyptian creation myths favor the resolution of opposites. The synthesizing forces of creation, represented by the neter Ptah, are aimed at maintaining human civilization. What is called "evil" in the world of humans did not exist in the world of the neters, and so we find instead a concept closer to chaos or disorder, represented by Seth.

Heka and Maat seem to participate in a similar resolution of opposites. Maat, representing cosmic order, truth, and justice, appeals to form and reason, reflecting attitudes of intellectual as well as emotional life. Maat, however, does not represent the love or justice found at our personal level. Rather, Maat's love and justice are on the scale of her cosmic unity. Quiet contemplation of this property of Maat may lead to comprehending her as a unifying force that we can then compare with Heka. To serve in this pairing with Maat, his magic must be equal in power to hers.

In the history of Western civilization great efforts have been made to describe magic as a force against the laws of nature. Our study of Heka shows that this is a false interpretation—at least from the ancient Egyptian point of view. Changing our perspective helps us to comprehend this alternative viewpoint. Versluis in *The Philosophy of Magic* emphasizes that the Egyptians considered magic an essential force of life, not a cause of phenomena in our world so much as an effect.[7] The notion that magic is a cause rather than an effect is commonly mistaken in the present day. This results from a general neglect of the concept of levels of phenomena in modern day Western society. The Egyptians believed that phenomena at levels higher than that of humans result in effects that we, in our ignorance of real causes, think overturn the normal laws of cause and effect. Keeping this distinction of cause and effect in mind, we can appreciate that with regard to magic, the power of the neters is only reflected in our world, not caused in it. To us, at our lower level, actions at higher levels are seen as an invasion that cannot occur "according to law." Instead of seeing such phenomena as magic expressing higher dimensions, we treat magic as an evil caused by imagined unlawful circumstances personified by a humanoid "devil."

Magic in the Pyramid Texts

As we noted earlier, modern scholars seem to avoid direct mention of Heka as neter of magic in their translations of the Pyramid Texts, but in a number of instances direct mention would make the meaning of the translations considerably easier to understand. In any case, we see the use of the word magic to signal that we are dealing with an influence that originates at the spiritual level of the world of the neters.*

The Pyramid Texts are a group of writings in hieroglyphs carved into the ceiling and walls of pyramids of the Old Kingdom from 2353 BCE to 2107 BCE. Beginning with the Pharaoh Unis at the end of the Fifth Dynasty, various compilations with slight variations of the Texts are found in pyramids through the Sixth Dynasty and one at the beginning of the Eighth Dynasty. In succession, these are the pyramids of Teti, Pepi I, Ankhesenpepi II (wife of Pepi I), Merenre, Pepi II, Neith (wife of Pepi I), Iput II (wife of Pepi), Wedjebetni (wife of Pepi II), and Ibi, a pharaoh of the Eighth Dynasty. Although Heka is not often recognized in the Pyramid Texts, magic is often mentioned.

In texts from the Pyramid of Unis, we find a reference to magic in what Allen (in *The Ancient Egyptian Pyramid Texts*) refers to as Recitation 211. The introduction reads:

---

*In what follows we refer to published translations that use the word *god,* but in our text we continue to use the Egyptian word *neter.*

"How beautiful is the sight, how pleasing the vision,"
say the gods, "of this god's going forth to the sky, of
Unis's going forth to the sky, with his bas atop him,
his ferocity at his sides, his magic at his feet.
Geb has acted for him just like he was acted for in the
same event."[8]

Ferocity is an attribute of Heka in all the Pyramid Texts and in the Book of Coming Forth by Day, where he is also named God of Magic. A related theme is found in the Pyramid Texts from Teti, having to do with his ascent to Nut. In Recitation 9, Teti is referred to as the doorkeeper of Horus and the gatekeeper of Osiris. His magic can "soothe" the wounds of Horus. He does this "with the magic that is in the gods when he first comes into being."[9] This provides further evidence that this magic is indeed an aspect of Heka in his role as one of the main principles of creation. In a text given in the Pyramid of Pepi I, Recitation 486, it is further pointed out that "the magic in the belly of Meryre belongs to him, as he emerges and ascends to the sky."[10] "Meryre" is a statue within the pyramid that represents the Pharaoh Pepi I in his effort to emerge and ascend, which requires the functioning of magic to be successful.

In an unrelated text from the Pyramid of Pepi I, Recitation 323, a great magical power is assigned directly to Pepi:

Tremble, sky; shake, earth—before this Pepi! Pepi is
Magic. Pepi is one who has magic.
This Pepi has come that this Pepi may akhify Orion,
that this Pepi might bring Osiris
to the fore, that this Pepi might put the gods on their
seats.[11]

In this case, not only is Pepi assigned the power of Heka, but the text also points out how, with the power of magic, the constellation of Orion is akhified (made into the highest spiritual order of gods) and thus understood to be the visible heavenly representation of Osiris, who is assisted by this great magic of Pepi to return to his seat. That Osiris had exchanged his original "seat" for his son, Horus, as King of the Living, as he himself, became King of Eternity, is stated in chapter 17 of the Book of Coming Forth by Day.

Further reference to the ferocity and magic of the pharaoh is made in the pyramids of Unis, Recitation 211 and Pepi I, Recitation 325. In the amplified version of Pepi I, proclamations are now made by Isis and Nephthys, rather than being attributed to the neters in general. They describe the role of Pharaoh Pepi as he goes forth surrounded by the magic of Heka and the important consequences of his becoming a neter. The text goes on to say:

> *"I shall get for you the gods who belong to the sky,"*
> *(says Isis), "and they will join for you the gods who*
> *belong to the earth, that you might exist with them*
> *and go on their arms."*
> *"I shall get for you the bas of Pe" (says*
> *Nephthys), "and the bas of Nekhen will be joined*
> *together for you."*
> *"Everything is for you—Geb is the one who*
> *argued for it with Atum, for it is what was done*
> *for him—and the Marshes of Reeds, the Horus*
> *Mounds and the Seth Mounds. Everything is for*
> *you: Geb is the one who argued for it with Atum,*
> *for it is what was done for him."*[12]

A further explication of the same text is given in the Pyramid of Pepi I, Recitation 512, and two variations come from the Pyramid of Pepi II, Recitations 422 and 430. Another version is given in the Pyramid of Merenre, Recitation 261. The Pyramid of Queen Neith, Recitation 11, contains a version in which the commentators are also Isis and Nephthys.

These variations are significant not only because of the magic described surrounding the pharaoh as neter, but also because they introduce the idea that each pharaoh, in his magical condition capable of "ascending," is important in the world of the neters due to his role of reconnecting the sky to the earth. In each case, the neter Geb, the neter of the earth, petitions Atum, the original neter of creation. The reunion of the representatives of sky and earth is equated with the union of the neters of Upper and Lower Egypt, Pe and Neken.

Rundle Clark points out and as we noted in chapter 2, splitting apart Nut and Geb introduced into the world the pain of separation. In the Pyramid Texts it is apparent that the magic of the ascending pharaoh plays the important function of removing this pain of separation by bringing about a reunification between the sky and the earth. It is in this sense that we use the modern psychological language of a "reconciliation of opposites." In this case the opposites were set up in the divine world by the act of creation, involving the sundering of the unity of the sky and the earth. The philosophically and psychologically important reconciliation of this original sundering is described in the Pyramid Texts as an act that is promoted by the magic of Heka.

We have not, however, exhausted the accounts that spell out all of the various attributes of Heka as the neter of magic. In fact, a somewhat different version of magic is given in Pepi I, Recitation 536, which reads:

> So, whoever shall [worship] Osiris and do this
> magic for him, he will be alive forever. Pepi is the
> one who worships you, Osiris, [Pepi] is the one
> who does [this] magic for you: [so he will be] alive
> forever.[13]

This is the only instance we know in which magic is specifically attributed the capacity of giving eternal life. However, it is of significance that in Unis Recitation 146 it is said of Unis,

Ho, Unis! You have not gone away dead: you have
gone away alive.[14]

Following this, Unis Recitation 153 says,

He has come to you, Red Crown; he has come to
you, Fiery One; he has come to you, Great One;
he has come to you, Great of Magic—clean for you
and fearful because of you.
    May you be content with him. . . .
    He has come to you, Great of Magic: for he
is Horus, encircled by the aegis [protection] of his
eye, the Great of Magic.[15]

In Unis Recitation 154, this message continues as:

Ho, Red Crown! Ho, Curl! Ho, Great One! Ho
    Great of Magic! Ho Fiery One,
May you make Unis's ferocity like your ferocity,
may you make this Unis's fearsomeness like
    your fearsomeness, . . .
may you make the love of this Unis like love
    of you.[16]

These recitations together establish not only that Unis was taken into the sky without having "died," but that Heka's powers in the spirit world are considerable. It is important to remember that these attributes of the neters are not in the physical world of our day-to-day lives, but are esoteric, dealing with our levels of higher consciousness.

In the Pyramid of Pepi II, however, there is a further explication of the theme of magic, this time also consisting of the magic attributed to the eye of Horus, which was seized by Seth in their prolonged battle. In

Pepi II Recitation 106–111, the power of magic is passed on to Pepi II in the verse "Osiris Pepi Neferkare, accept Horus's eye, of which you said: 'Its magic is greater than mine.'"

We reach this conclusion because in the Pyramid Texts of Pepi II, on the occasion of his ascent, he is given the name Osiris Pepi Neferkare. The name Osiris is a formula assigned in the Book of Coming Forth by Day to the person being transformed, and it specifies that he or she has become a candidate for eternal life, ruled by Osiris in the Duat. It is thus this "dead" Pepi II who is granted the title Great of Magic. Following this, in Pepi II Recitation 531, the great god Djehuti is called "Lord of Magic." Furthermore, in the Pyramid of Queen Neith Recitation 225, it says:

> Horus has made your magic great in your identity
> of Great of Magic. You are the great god. . . .
>   You are in control of the Nile Valley through
> this Horus through whom you exercise control;
> you are in control of the Delta through this Horus
> through whom you exercise control. You shall
> exercise control and defend your body from your
> opponent.[17]

Pepi II is thus greeted as ruler of a united Upper and Lower Egypt, in a union that appears to take place in the world of the Duat, which in figure 7.3 on page 182 is shown to be encircled by the body of Osiris at the top. Indications that the "departed" Pharoah has entered the Duat do not occur in the earlier Pyramid Texts of Unis, Teti, Pepi I, or Merenre. We are not certain whether this is an intentional difference among the texts, but there appears to be little in the Pyramid Texts that is stated casually.

In the verse found in several pyramids as Pepi I Recitation 62, Merenre Recitation 52, Pepi II Recitation 322, and Neith Recitation 227 the neter Geb, who is responsible for having spoken to Atum in the interests of healing the scission between the sky and the earth, is in his role as the eldest son of Shu, the neter who originally carried out the separation of Nut and Geb, long before the creation of humans. Figure 7.5 shows Heka in the traditional place of Shu in the act of lifting Nut to her position in the sky, hence separating her from Geb, the neter of earth.[18] This demonstrates the relatively high level of Heka in the hierarchy of the neters. In this verse found in multiple pyramids, the Pharaoh who has become Osiris in "death" is presented to Geb. The text reads:

> Gather him to you, that [what is against him] might end.
>
> You alone are the great god, for Atum has given you his inheritance. He has given you the Ennead gathered, and Atum himself as well amongst them, gathered for his senior son's son in you, for he has seen you effective, your heart big (with pride); persuasive in your identity of the persuasive mouth, the god's elite one; standing on the earth and judging at the fore of the Ennead, your fathers and mothers . . . .
>
> You are the lord of the entire earth, in control of the Ennead and every god as well. . . . You are the god who controls all the gods, for the eye has emerged in your head as the Nile-Valley Great-of-Magic Crown, the eye has emerged in your head as the Delta Great-of-Magic Crown, Horus has followed you and desired you, and you are apparent as the Dual King in control of the gods and their kas as well."[19]

It is of particular interest to note that when either Heka or Shu is shown holding up the sky, their arms are bent at the elbows and extended upward in the same form that is used in hieroglyphs to

*Figure 7.5. Heka, the neter personifying magic, in the place
of Shu, lifting Nut supported on each side by images of the
ka with arms raised. Twenty-first Dynasty coffin.
From Naydler,* Temple of the Cosmos, *figure 3.13.*

represent the sound ka (figure 7.5). The supporting bird images also
extend their arms up in the same manner. The ka, represented by the
glyph of the upraised arms bent at the elbow, is the Egyptian name
for the soul that is created by Khnum on his potter's wheel at the
same time as the material pharaoh is created for birth in the human
world. That is, this ka, created by Khnum, is intimately related to the
function of the pharaoh, perhaps by lifting the human soul toward
celestial or spiritual influences in the same way that Heka and Shu
lift the sky above earth.

In a number of illustrations of the theme the arms are supported at
the elbows by rams. In Egyptian, the word for *ram* is pronounced ba,
the name used to describe the next higher level of the soul than the ka.
Ba is thus a further aspect of the developing soul that is on its way to

becoming spirit, or akh, a state of spiritual being that shines forth like the sun, Ra.

We would like to draw attention to Pepi I Recitation 486, where it is pointed out that the characteristics of all the various neters are incorporated as "limbs" and other body parts of Pepi Meryre as he ascends through the sky. It states:

> *The magic that appertains to me is that which is in*
> *my belly; . . .*[20]

It goes on to say that if any god fails to help "lay down a stairway" by which Pepi can ascend, he will have no benefit from the whole process of transformation that will take place. The text continues:

> *This Pepi is not the one who says this against*
> *you gods: magic [Heka] is the one that says this*
> *against you gods. Meryre is the one who belongs*
> *to the mound that has magic, as he emerges and*
> *ascends to the sky.*
>
> *Any god who will lay down a stairway for*
> *Pepi as he emerges and Meryes ascends to the*
> *sky, and any god who will provide his seat in the*
> *great boat as he emerges and this Pepi ascends*
> *to the sky, the earth will be hacked up for him, a*
> *deposited offering will be laid down before him, a*
> *bowl shall be made for him . . .*
>
> *Any god who will receive the arm of this*
> *Meryre to the sky when he has gone to*
> *Horus's enclosure in the Cool Waters, his ka*
> *will be justified before Geb.*[21]

In summary, the Pyramid Texts indicate that magic is not only inherent in the creation of the neters as inheritors of the greatness of

Atum, but that it also penetrates the human world, including the affairs of the pharaohs of Egypt and those who are ruled.

The Need for Attention and the Role of Magic

It is relevant to our consideration of magic to make further reference here to a related power that is necessary for our individual internal perception. Kingsley writes extensively on the Ancient Greek concept of *mêtis*.[22] The word was used by the earliest Greeks as the name of the titan Mêtis. The Greek gods Oceanus and Tethys gave birth to the goddess Mêtis, and thus she is of an earlier age than even Zeus. She was the first spouse of Zeus and mother of his first daughter, Athena. She was said to be both a threat to and an indispensable aid to Zeus, and her name connotes both the "magical cunning" of the trickster Prometheus and the "royal mêtis" of Zeus. The Orphic tradition enthroned Mêtis side by side with Eros as primal cosmogonic forces. Plato made Poros, or "creative ingenuity," the child of Mêtis.[23]

Kingsley presents mêtis as "the particular quality of intense alertness that can be effortlessly aware of everything else at once."[24] He points out that such alertness requires a good deal of magic and trickery to avoid the illusory distractions of life. It offers the principal route to what the earliest Greek philosophers, in their prepared state, considered necessary for a balanced contact with the sacred impulses that maintain life. He says that mêtis is at the origin of "a teaching to make sure that no illusory person with any illusory tricks in this illusory world will ever manage to outwit or get the better of him [the observer]."[25] That is, only as long as we can individually exercise the ultimate property of attention and discrimination, resulting from our exercise of mêtis within ourselves, will we have the power to distinguish our real existence from the illusory that we take to be our daily lives.

Parmenides, in a poem translated and interpreted by Kingsley, points out that the lack of the power of discrimination in our illusory world underlies our difficulty in understanding life. Parmenides travels to the "depths of darkness at the furthest the edges of existence,"[26] which is very reminiscent of the Sumerian netherworld and Egyptian Duat. In that realm he is directly instructed by a goddess on the challenges of seeing his real world and the need for mêtis before sending him back to his ordinary life.

Parmenides learns that it takes a bit of magic and trickery to keep one's attention from being distracted. It is clear from the special conditions of Parmenides' travel and from the actions and attitudes of his "successor," Empedocles, that this advice to develop discrimination is not related to any ordinary wariness that we might try to cultivate. In fact, Parmenides' instructions coming from a goddess point out that this effort of attention could only emanate from the level of the gods. These god-like powers serve as the foundation for the sacred undertaking that was learned through incubation of the initiate in the course of worship of Apollo.

Our present day difficulty with recognizing the power of such ancient practices lies in our modern Western sensibilities that are heavily weighted toward the rational. We have trouble ensuring that our own sense of discrimination is at the intended level without recognizing the necessary role of mêtis or magic in our efforts.

We have been given ample evidence of the need for the transcendent power of magic in the translations of the Pyramid Texts. Following the reasoning of Versluis, we can appreciate that while the effects of magic may appear to us at our level of perception, they must originate from an esoteric power of discrimination that arises from the gods. These magical effects can be transformative; they require of us in the human world special efforts to understand.[27] Those who are unprepared cannot hope to comprehend the appropriate levels of higher attention.

Parmenides' warnings about contentment with a superficial level of understanding may have originated in Egypt and been passed on to him in ways unknown. In fact, it is important to note that Parmenides and Empedocles both belonged to traditions that can be traced to Homeric times (circa the fifth century BCE). Borrowing important concepts from the Egyptians would account for the glowing accounts of the later Greek philosophers, who extolled the secrets they encountered in the Egyptian temples when they were first taught the stories of creation described in chapter 2. The Greeks also honored the secrecy demanded of them by this teaching.

A heightened self-awareness is certainly required where strange gods or objects symbolize perceptions that are unfamiliar in our cultural memories. We have presented a number of examples in this book. The difficulties that Gilgamesh encountered in his search for immortality direct our attention to a number of hard to recognize but credible distinctions between the Land of the Living, where we experience our life, and the Land of Utnapishtim, where we might, with Gilgamesh, seek help in reaching the objects of our aspirations. The preparation and continued attention of the pharaoh as he travels through the Duat and deals with its many challenges is another example. The two trees in the Garden of Eden suggest a parallel symbolism that requires fine discrimination to unlock. Kingsley points out how both Parmenides and Empedocles taught that sharp discernment is not an automatic skill.[28] Special openness, particularly engaging that magical quality he calls "mêtis," is needed if we are not to find ourselves immediately assigning the unfamiliar to pre-established categories. Such openness is, to quote a friend, "no cheap thing."

The search for higher consciousness can start only from realizing a sense of something missing or recognizing a need for what we do not understand—something internal and real in the present. It cannot be supposed that the searcher, figuratively fumbling in the dark, can know what is sought or what might be found. What is required is a freedom or openness to other influences. Once this openness has been achieved, one can appreciate that what needs to be learned does not come from the symbols of the ancients. In fact, it is unlikely to be found within the myths. Rather, it must be found within the whole of our personal experience of life. Many of us are fortunate to have tasted higher energy within ourselves during fleeting moments throughout our lives. Understanding becomes possible once one can consider them as glimpses of what might be called eternity and wholeness. These come to us when we participate in that extra dimensionality of being that, for want of a better term, we call the higher consciousness within us—the Self.

In this way, the alchemists fortify the lesson of the myths that the recognition of the meaning of life involves some essential, qualitative process of change that is so profound that our view of ourselves must undergo a transformation. We discover that the search for higher consciousness leads not to the stars, but to ourselves.

The Relationship between Heka and Maat

We have recounted the characteristics of Heka as magic for two reasons. First, Heka and Maat, in the Egyptian worldview, were initially regarded as a pair of opposites that must find reconciliation. Second, after Atum created these first two principles, he became aware of himself.

If magic is the equivalent of the religion of the Egyptians, the greatness of Heka's power becomes clearer to us. Such power is hard to conceive in the Western world with its history of sectarian religions, but given the evidence of the Pyramid Texts, which are the first written texts of Egypt, we see the remarkable power of magic. Such incredible power must be balanced. We find the requisite balance in the attributes of Maat. Perhaps the power of Maat could be understood from her description as the neter of cosmic unity alone. But knowing that she is also truth and justice, we conceive in her a strength and breadth that we would find difficult to comprehend were it not for her juxtaposition with the awesome power of Heka. Because Heka as magic underlies the seemingly limitless process of creation, it must be reconciled with forces of a similar scale, such as those of Maat. She allows this remarkable created world to achieve a state of organization that affects the purpose of life itself.

Heka and Maat act throughout all levels of the worlds of both neters and humans. Pharaohs, who were considered the embodiment of the great neter Horus, were judged on the extent to which they satisfied the properties of Maat. Her significance in this regard lends insight into how Egyptians perceived the need to balance ultimate power with cosmic unity, truth, and justice. It was believed that the pharaohs' actions in this world would have consequences in the Duat and beyond.

This chapter directly affirms that all the transformative processes we have been told of indeed emanate from the underlying influence of magic and order as personified by the Egyptian neters Heka and Maat, the two primary principles of creation. As Naydler points out, "Heka is the power by which the spiritual becomes manifest, for he is the connecting link between the Godhead, Atum, and all that comes from Atum."[29] Heka is thus the divine creative power that exists in both the spiritual and material worlds and is the means through which these spiritual and material levels of existence connect with each other. In this way it appears the powers of union that in our time have been reserved for what is called "religion" (a word that originally meant to "link" or to "bind together") are in these texts clearly associated with the magic that, ironically, for at least three hundred years since the end of the Spanish Inquisition has been denied a place in the Christian West.

The special forces of magic, personified as Heka, and of cosmic unity, truth, and justice, personified by Maat, jointly enable us to understand new and unfamiliar characteristies that seem to be necessary at the levels of existence. Certain myths—such as those involving Enlil and Enki, Adam and Ashah, Gilgamesh and Enkidu, Osiris and Isis—show us that achieving the right level of awareness allows for the necessary reconciliation of opposites that is critical to awakening higher consciousness.

The Need to Awaken to the Larger View of Reality

Our introduction points out that consciousness is the foundation on which humankind tries to build a case for having a unique and special place among the creatures of the earth. Consciousness enables us to observe various impulses of energy within us as drives toward intended ends. We are able to see the desires of our animal instincts. At the same time, we see aspirations toward a finer nature to which our knowledge directs us. Our ability to discern the difference between our ordinary being and our higher levels of functioning sometimes leads us to suppose that we can make objective judgments about our behavior and our perceptions. We rely on this discernment to help us discover what is real. Our hope of discovering this reality is an important beginning step in ascertaining the ultimate purpose of our lives.

We must, however, discover in this process what can enable us to perceive our personal situation in relation to any ideal. There cannot be any hope that this can come from any ordinary level of perception. We seek a new level of being, one that lies beyond our present experiences; and we have only direct experience to guide our search. We must begin by cultivating a wider point of view of our circumstances than is customary for us. It is in this process that we encounter difficulties with our ideals. What passes for conscious awareness is all too easily confused with functions that are more an expression of our illusions than our wisdom. The subjective, sometimes dreamy, sometimes anxious states in which we compare ourselves with others—What do they think of us? How do our circumstances compare with theirs? Do they appreciate how hard we work or how tired we get? Do they see how much we value them, even when our own efforts are not appreciated?—are far removed from the perspective that is afforded by our rare insights and limited direct experiences of our personal situation. We do not require great knowledge to appreciate that speculation, anxiety, and daydreaming contribute nothing to our stature as human beings.

Direct experience is when we are consciously aware of ourselves in the things we see and do. We have seen it in the echoes of direct experience that speak to us out of the great works of art and literature of past or present ages. Direct experience enables us to verify the reality of our search and speaks to us of the essential unity of humans throughout the ages. It enables us to understand that the expressions of the finer spirits have always been the same. It is the real basis for understanding one another, and for hoping to understand together what we know as wisdom. In this sense myths are among the great works of art. Myths guide us toward understanding insights that come from our direct experience but that would be almost impossible to evaluate without them. The mysterious and unknown authors of the myths have understood what stands in the way of the free exchange of energies on which our real growth and development depend. Because of this, they lead us to appreciate our need to be awakened to a different, more immediate level of perception.

For this reason it seems important to acknowledge that an element of tragedy is expressed in all these myths. Adam's attempts to find knowledge taught him of death and led to his "banishment" from Eden. Gilgamesh's feats of daring led to the death of his dearest and closest friend, and his profound suffering led to his subsequent search for immortality and the eventual denial of everything he had sought. In Egypt, the creation of a marvelous civilization by Osiris and Isis led to the murder and dismemberment of Osiris, and only after many more struggles did his resurrection take place in the land of the everlasting.

Are personal tribulation and pain, as is implied in the myths, essential parts of gaining wisdom? Life experiences that have given us a taste of what we consider the nature of our higher consciousness have left quite a different impression: brief but vivid feelings of well-being on a sunny spring day; a breath of fresh air from the sea; sudden pleasure when one bites into a sweet and juicy orange. These are moments of enlivenment that most of us have known in one form or another and that we value.

It is true that we have also experienced the opposite. At times it is difficult to imagine being genuinely free of the limitations, tensions, and anxieties in life. We have little desire to remember moments of empty loneliness or of being drained of all vitality following an emotional upheaval. We are not naive enough to suppose that a taste of the higher consciousness is found only in moments of ecstasy. We know enough about tragedy to understand its dramatic value in works of literature. But is this a necessary part of the process of discovering wisdom?

Final Comments

What seems most evident from life experiences is that at any one time our viewpoint is relatively narrow. Our sense of balance spans only small dimensions and short durations. When we identify with moments of pleasure, we avoid glimpses of a lack of worth or sensitivity. In moments of depression, we may feel that real happiness never existed. Dismal "adult" emotions may compare unfavorably with what we remember encountering as children, with a child's natural flexibility and depth of feeling. The child and the adult both experience pleasure and pain, but where the child may bounce emotionally from low to high, the adult becomes trapped in a tangle of memories where sadness becomes enmeshed in self-pity and anguish keeps company with anger.

Awakening to the imbalances of our world provides a new standpoint from which to view oneself. But it is necessarily an awakening to the facts of separations and compartmentalizations, the partiality of our usual views of existence. Whether happy or sad, these small views are surely tragic in relation to the vast potential of life. Before people who would be wise can present themselves at the doors of the wise individual, they must awaken to the reality of their partiality. The primary purpose of the myths is to urge us to awaken. The wonder is that they seem to be so difficult to hear.

The myths also speak of the need for struggle. We are familiar with the Christian idea of struggle against evil. However, all the myths emphasize a special aspect of evil for humankind. They repeatedly point out that the real evil for us is isolation and the separation of parts. Using symbolism, they also show that under the ordinary circumstances of life the desire for individuality leads to isolation. When one's desire becomes the opposite of what is needed to achieve wholeness, transformation is blocked. Isolation leads to enmity and division, while integration leads to positive relationships and wholeness. The struggle in life is the work of embracing and reconciling opposites: love-hate, joy-sadness, hope-despair, and so forth.

The Egyptian story of the struggle between Horus and Seth is of particular importance in this regard. This struggle between gods seems on a different scale than those of Gilgamesh in the Land of the Living or Adam in the Garden of Eden. There is no hint of the bravado of Gilgamesh or the naïveté of Adam in this celestial struggle. In fact, the symbolism implies that in this battle even a temporary victory could not be sustained without the cooperation of Isis. Our attention is rightly attracted to the drama of the struggle in which the forces of entropy and decay continually beset Horus. But the gods cannot destroy one another. They can only restrain with the help of the guardian Isis. A unique feature of this battle is that it never comes to an end. There is no final resolution. At one point the gods simply agree that other matters need attention.

This provides an interesting insight into the dynamism that activates our internal and external worlds. In this struggle among gods we are obliquely shown that the need is not for the conquest of one side by the other; there is always the continuous engagement in desperate struggle. Rather, there is a requirement for resolution of opposites only possible through alertness to the whole. This attention alone can prevent us from being overwhelmed by the forces of partiality and strife that separate us from the obligatory interdependencies of life.

So here at the end of our exploration, we hope that readers will see these myths in a new light that will contribute to their explorations of themselves and of the world around them—to help them find and establish a stronger Self within themselves. Throughout this book, the myths have been shown to address profound questions concerning the nature of reality. The creation myths we have uncovered can be viewed as creation of the external world only by literalists living in naïveté. Do we recognize our inability to discriminate between our reactions to external stimuli, as opposed to internal feelings? Do we know how to distinguish the Egyptian concepts of the Everlasting from the Eternal? Plato brings up a serious question about the nature of life and death in the Gorgias dialogue when he quotes Euripides' famous inquiry: "Who knows if life be death, and if death be life?"[30]

The Sumerian and Egyptian myths directly influenced the Judaic culture and formed the basis of some Old Testament stories, which, in turn, influenced present-day Western culture. That is, we in the West can trace our cultural roots directly to myths written down some 4,500 years ago! But the challenges modern societies face lie in understanding what these myths are telling us and determining how we can make use of them in our everyday life to awaken our higher consciousness.

APPENDIX 1

THE LINEAGE OF MYTH

The creation myths of the Middle East and Egypt are far older than their written forms would suggest. According to Budge,[1] the earliest Egyptian myths in the Book of Coming Forth by Day originate from stories that must have been told orally and illustrated before the Fifth Dynasty of Egypt, in the mid-third millennium BCE. For example, the Egyptian myth of Osiris was apparently never fully written down in any language until it was transcribed into Greek by Plutarch, who visited Egypt from Greece in the first century CE. Throughout the earlier period, before 3500 BCE to 1000 BCE, the Egyptians' popular understanding of the stories must have depended largely on the illustrations and the rituals that accompanied their recital in public celebrations.

The flowering of the Sumerian culture took place around 3,000 BCE.[2] Sumerian myths followed an evolution similar to the Egyptian, starting as oral stories long before they were written in cuneiform in 2700 BCE. Frankfort points out that the earliest cylinder seals depicted scenes from daily life.[3] Only later, perhaps in the early years of the second millennium, were mythic themes extensively developed. The myths are well represented on the cylinder seals in common use of the period.

In choosing and presenting myth we have taken pains to find the very earliest forms. To approach the very earliest meanings of the myths and to understand these ancient societies requires a breadth of view that encompasses their rituals, texts, architecture, and other cultural elements. In this appendix we attempt to provide the reader with insights into the lineage of the myths we use in the book built on all of these tools.

The Egyptian Lineage

Egyptian mythology is relatively uniform and recognizable over long periods in the texts and figures written on walls of pyramids, temples, and tombs, and even inscribed on mummy wrappings. The original hieroglyphic texts tend to be well known and repeated faithfully from place to place, but that is not to say that there were no changes over time.

The writing in Old Egyptian hieroglyphs used to record the Pyramid Texts in the pyramids in the Fifth and Sixth Dynasties, circa 2300 BCE, has an especial clarity and beauty. Modern scholars have discerned their meaning with the help of fragments of the extensive ceremonial figures that lined the once-enclosed pathway leading from the Valley Temple on the banks of the Nile up to the pyramid.[4]

In the subsequent Sixth Dynasty, pharaohs were commemorated in the pyramids of Saqqara with written texts, which are extensively enhanced in nearby temple chambers with stories depicted in the beautifully carved or painted images.

The much later Twelfth Dynasty structures, circa 2000 BCE, housed in the Karnak Temple Complex, used a similar technique of both texts and images. This continued into the two main Eighteenth Dynasty temples, circa 1500 BCE, one at Karnak and one at Luxor. Other important sources of written and pictorial materials from this time period are carved and painted in passageways and chambers of the tombs of the Eighteenth to Twenty-second Dynasty pharaohs in the Valley of the Kings, across the river from Luxor proper. Interpretation of Egyptian imagery plays an essential role in our modern understanding of the often terse or enigmatic written texts.

Translations of the Egyptian Book of Coming Forth by Day have been widely known since they were first published in both hieroglyphic form and English by Budge in the last years of the nineteenth century.[5] Budge misnamed it the Book of the Dead, following Lepsius, who in 1867 used the German term Todtenbuchs for texts discovered before the first Pyramid Texts were found and translated. Faulkner's translations used the Book of Going Forth by Day as well as the Pyramid Texts.[6] Faulkner's later translations have been of great value, even though they do not include the images that are an informative part of Budge's translations. Even more recently, Ashby uses the more proper name the Book of Coming Forth by Day, which is the title we use here.[7]

Budge points out that the very earliest Egyptian "sacred" writing refers to early versions of these texts, although for his own publications he uses revised and amplified texts written on papyri or on mummy wrappings from the much more recent New Kingdom, together with the illustrations that accompanied them. Also particularly useful are the Book of Gates, whose texts and scenes are inscribed on the walls of the tomb of Ramses I (Nineteenth Dynasty) and Ramses VI (Twentieth Dynasty), and the Book of What Is in the Duat, whose texts and scenes are inscribed in full on the walls of the tomb of Tuthmosis III (Eighteenth Dynasty).[8] One panel is shown in figure A1.1. By the New Kingdom of the Eighteenth Dynasty, the Book of Coming Forth by Day included extensive commentaries added by the priesthood, marked by phrases such as "What then is this?" or "As others say." In all cases, the translations are made clearer by reference to the many inscriptions and symbolic figurations that accompany almost all the texts. As is persuasively demonstrated by Naydler, it would often be difficult, if not impossible, to understand the textual symbolism without the accompanying images.[9]

The main differences among the modern-day translations of the Egyptian texts, and they are quite substantial, are a result of varying interpretations by modern translators. There is a distinct difference in tone between the translations of Budge and much of the more recent material. Recent linguists and translators hold Budge's versions to be woefully outdated;[10] however, in our eyes, Faulkner's translations of

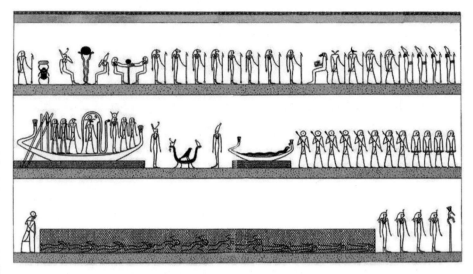

Figure A1.1. Tenth Hour of the Book of What Is in the Duat, from the tomb of Tuthmosis III. From West, Serpent in the Sky.

the Pyramid Texts—which do not include illustrations—are sometimes completely unintelligible.[11] More recently, a version published and illustrated by Naydler demonstrates the advantages of an author having an appreciation of the environment in which Egyptian beliefs developed.[12] J. P. Allen's book *The Ancient Egyptian Pyramid Texts* updates the full collection of texts from ten Old Kingdom pyramids.[13] We use Allen as it is the most comprehensive collection, and he provides a full concordance table for the use of anyone interested in referring to the other collections.

It is also essential to reference the major work of R. A. Schwaller de Lubicz, *Le Temple de l'homme* (*The Temple of Man*).[14] Schwaller and his wife, Isha Schwaller de Lubicz, spent decades in Egypt exploring the Ancient Egyptian culture. In his book *The Temple of Man* he presents an exhaustive exposition of Egyptian mathematics, geometry, architecture, and art. In doing so he gains insights into the cultural and spiritual underpinnings of the ancient Egyptians. He shows how differently they approached life. From his work they are seen to view the world as an eternal, creative whole with a unifying life force.

The Sumerian Lineage

Similarly, for the Sumerian myths, we must draw on the translated texts as well as images. While we have access to a number of translated texts, many others remain untranslated. Unfortunately, in contrast to the historical record in Egypt, we have only limited and secondary information about Sumerian rituals. We draw on the available Sumerian, and subsequent Babylonian, materials to explore the nature of the information the Mesopotamian myths contain. In doing so, it is important to note that the wedge-shaped Sumerian cuneiform script is totally different from the alphabetic Semitic language in which the later Babylonian versions were written. Mitchell points out that "Sumerian is a non-Semitic language unrelated to any other that we know, and is as distant from Akkadian as Chinese is from English."[15]

Johnson points out, in relation to the Mesopotamian myths, that the earlier Sumerian culture transitioned into a quite distinct later Babylonian culture through "development of the basic institutions of 'civilization' . . . the growth of cities; the specialization of labor; the hierarchy of rulers, intellectuals and priests; the development of written records, libraries, courts of justice, measurement, astronomy; a common calendar; and a rich literature more than a thousand years before the Bible or the Iliad. It was the function of myth and ritual to bind the rich farmland of the rural areas to the capital city, and to bind the city to the temple, the palace, and the deified ruler. The primary role of the New-Year festival was to harmonize the cycles of earth, rural and urban, with the cycles of heaven."[16] This highlights the importance of the myth to the society over a very long span, before 3000 BCE to 1600 BCE, in parallel with the Egyptian culture.

For the Sumerian myths, Dalley, working with only written texts, points out that the written forms in which we have the various versions of the Sumerian myths may be quite different, both in their outline and in their thematic emphasis.[17] The subject matter included in a late rendering of a text may entirely leave out one of the more central themes of an earlier version. In her opinion, some differences may be explained by the fact that not all versions were intended to be read to audiences; some are in the form of aides-mémoire, or summaries. In these documents, parts of the myth might be sketched in outline, while clearly important events may be referred to elliptically if at all. These short versions were used to assist reciters, to prompt teachers, to recruit entertainers, and even to record particular presentations. In keeping with this view, she notes that some of the earliest Sumerian versions of a myth may give us a rather longer and more complete form than the later versions, which appear in various languages (largely without illustrations) in the libraries of the second millennium BCE. As authors, we have found the need to maintain flexibility in our approach to their study, not placing undue reliance on any one version. We attempt to keep our view of what is said in the various sources as open as possible, without sacrificing attention to trends and without missing the deliberate alterations that arose in the various societies where the myths appeared.

In Mesopotamia, we see the continuing interest that the ancients took in their legends through the many copies of the cuneiform text that have been found throughout the area. The story of Gilgamesh was copied and recopied over a period of nearly two thousand years, from the third-millennium BCE text fragments found in the remains of the very early Sumerian culture of ancient Mesopotamia to the most complete edition, an Akkadian Semitic version found at Nineveh from the seventh-century BCE library of Assurbanipal, last king of the Assyrian Empire, written on twelve cuneiform tablets.

Some of the Mesopotamian myths known to us as rather extensive epics, such as the Epic of Gilgamesh with its story of the Flood, may have begun as shorter stories dealing with specific topics. The original eleventh tablet of this myth contains what is called the Chaldean account of the Flood. Significant fragments of the story of the Flood have been found at second millennium sites of the Hittite Empire in Anatolia, written in Semitic Akkadian. A Canaanite version was excavated from sites at Sultantepe in southern Turkey, and a Palestinian version from Megiddo.

The many parallels between the Mesopotamian story of the Flood and the later Hebrew and Christian stories make it apparent that the Hebrews modeled their story on the earlier version. They may have adopted it from their Babylonian captors or from a source that the Babylonians also used, all of which descended from the writings of the Sumerians.

Whichever path provided the transmission of the story, the Flood presented in the Bible is accepted by many as being derived from the *Epic of Gilgamesh,* a work that was known in the third millennium BCE, more than two thousand years before the Old Testament was composed.

Many different shorter tales, especially among the noncosmogonic, may have been utilized as oral storytelling material as part of the evening entertainment for commercial caravans in their increasingly extensive expeditions through the Middle East. Dalley believes that some versions of Mesopotamian myths found in excavations bear evidence of "competition" literature.[18] She uses this term to describe situations in which storytellers, who regularly joined caravans in journeys over the deserts and took part in long sea voyages, were invited to vie with one another for the interests of their captive audiences. Records must have been kept of the stories that were particularly valued.

Our attention has been drawn especially to Mitchell's version of the Gilgamesh legend; he reviewed seven previous translations in the process of producing it.[19] Among the most important of the scholarly efforts for Mitchell is a modern English edition that includes both transliteration and cuneiform versions of the text written by George.[20] Mitchell points out that the account accepted by scholars as the standard version of this epic was produced some five hundred years before the story discovered at Nineveh (dating to about 650 BCE), but much later than the Sumerian fragments that still exist and were used in chapters 2 and 3. This "ancestor" of the Gilgamesh epic is known as the Old Babylonian version and was written in Akkadian. It paraphrases some of the earlier Sumerian stories, which tell parts of the story of Gilgamesh and

Enkidu, and includes Sumerian stories we have discussed that are not an integral part of the Gilgamesh epic.

Mitchell also points out that the Old Babylonian version is not really the basis for the story as we now have it because that version is very fragmentary. Instead, we have a translation produced by a scholar-priest named Sin-leqi-unninni, who elaborated on the Old Babylonian version some five hundred years after it was produced. His writing is now referred to by scholars as the standard version. Mitchell calls Sin-leqi-unninni a conservative editor, in that most of his translations, where it is possible to check the original, copy it line for line, with no changes in vocabulary or word order. However, with the unavoidable fragmentations, resulting in lost text, he ventures into expansions that show him to be an original poet. We are indebted to his intelligence and creativity, for they have assisted our understanding of the effect that such an important myth has had on our heritage.

Mitchell's version is a refreshing new account representing a change in the general level of our understanding of ancient myths in recent years. To some his work will appear brash. We therefore need to recognize a new sense of value being shown in recent times. Advances in our understanding better reflect the ancient community of seekers who composed the Sumerian and Egyptian myths. No longer do we talk of ancient Egyptians as writing in "spells."*

The Potential for Shared Influences

Central to our study of myth is the book by Giorgio de Santillana and Hertha von Dechend titled *Hamlet's Mill*.[21] They provide a clear argument for an in-depth astronomical knowledge by ancient societies that has become a major source of information for subsequent cultures right up until today. For example, the sexagesimal system—which is the basis of the current system of degrees, minutes, and seconds of arc in

---

*The Electronic Text Corpus of Sumerian Literature (ETCSL) provides a full on-line version of the Sumerian texts at http://etcsl.orinst.ox.ac.uk.

the measurement of circles; the description of navigational geographic coordinates; and the measurement of time—is now recognized as a Sumerian invention for measuring angular changes in the position of astral bodies.

De Santillana and von Dechend demonstrate that the gods associated with the various constellations appear in the myths of Egypt and Mesopotamia. Further, these myths symbolically describe the relations among the stars, the planets, the sun, and the moon in their daily, monthly, annual, and precessional cycles in the skies. While we may never fully understand the extent to which these astronomic events shaped the ancient myths, there can be no doubt that they were a major factor.

Making Use of the Ancient in Modern Times

We have no particular expertise or objective basis for identifying the precise date of the first formulation of these myths. The subject is still a matter of debate among archaeologists and religionists whose special area of study is the geographic area of concern to us. Frankfort's interpretation of the data, however, based on his wide experience, provides a reassuring guide for exploring this information. In particular, he points out that there is strong evidence for early (predynastic) exchanges between Egypt and Mesopotamia, but goes on to say, "comparison between [them] discloses, not only that writing, representational art, monumental architecture, and a new kind of political coherence were introduced in the two countries; it also reveals the striking fact that the purpose of their writing, the contents of their representations, the functions of their monumental buildings, and the structure of their new societies differed completely. What we observe is not merely the establishment of civilized life, but the emergence, concretely, of the distinctive 'forms' of Egyptian and Mesopotamian civilization."[22]

Ancient knowledge is not often well preserved through the long periods of disorder that follow the decline of a society. The ancient

Sumerian culture was not even recognized as a distinct entity until the latter part of the nineteenth century CE. Kramer[23] points out that it was not until the writings of Oppert in 1869 that scholars accepted the suspicion of Rawlinson[24] that an entirely unknown non-Semitic language existed. Considerable progress has been made over the past half-century in finding resolutions for the sometimes vigorous debates over the translation and interpretation of the fragmentary evidence. Much of what has been found in official archaeological expeditions has now been carefully catalogued, and much of it is also published in forms that allow comparison by scholars. Initially these scholars were from the European nations that sponsored the excavations. However, interest developed in North America by the late nineteenth century and, in recent years, spread increasingly to various Asian centers with particular interest displayed by the nationals of the modern states in which the ancient ruins are still being excavated.

The spreading interest has encouraged excavators on many fronts, and inevitably, with time, substantial numbers of new fragments have appeared in the hands of commercial dealers, who have bought them from the original sellers or their representatives, and eventually sold them to the professionals. While some of these fragments have supplied vital information, the translators may be unable to establish the exact provenance of the materials themselves. The very proliferation of sources has added new work of examining and matching complementary fragments, or matching them with illustrations from various places. Ironically, parallel with this proliferation of source material has also come a proliferation of information, analyses, and discussions through the Internet, such as on the ETCSL site. Information of varying quality is made readily available there and is subject to varying degrees of synthesis and interpretation. This imposes a new requirement for discrimination on the part of readers that was not so evident in relation to more conventional, published scholarly efforts.

We can illustrate the kind of problem that can appear by drawing a parallel with the difficulty in confirming and releasing to the public the newly found and newly translated versions of books from the Old and New Testaments of the Bible. It was not until the mid-1900s that highly significant new sources for this venerated literature were found, both in Palestine and in Egypt. Preservation, translation, and interpretation of the new finds have occupied many experts, the results of whose efforts are only now, a half-century or more later, becoming widely known.

An important new perspective on what had initially been accepted as original, even inspired texts has resulted, generating controversy among both individuals and institutions. This is of particular interest for us because it demonstrates deep interest in spiritual matters in our Western society, despite the fact that it is largely secular in its outlook. It clearly speaks to us of the need for an open mind in attempting to arrive at a sense of original intentions.

The myths used here introduce questions and ideas about the origin and nature of the world, the arising of the gods, and the way they created and interacted with humans. It is of critical importance to current audiences that we see these creations and interactions as occurring within us—not in some external fairy-tale land. Through the myths, whole communities, perhaps at widely separated places throughout this ancient world, found a commonality of outlook that was important background for the arising of various religions. The stories themselves must have been repeated many times in different circumstances, and became widely known before they were written into the literature, which now affords us a chance to hear the tenor of the original aspirations. These stories incorporate important lessons about our inner self that were preserved for generations. This preservation may have been a stronger motive for the invention of writing than the more commonly acknowledged motive of keeping tally in early commerce.

We believe that recognition and communication of what is gradually being brought to light by these efforts results in new opportunities for making use of ancient knowledge. Recognition of the state of preparation of those who have supplied recent translations will be clear to all who are able to follow the lineage of the transcriptions over time. As an example, the recent publications by Naydler (*Shamanic Wisdom of the Pyramid Texts*) and Allen (*The Ancient Egyptian Pyramid Texts*) on the Pyramid Texts get a lot of meaning out of the order and location of the specific texts within the Pyramid complex. Without such knowledge of the flow of the corpus, much of our present understanding would be lost.

However, in addition to carefully adding new translations of ancient lore to our pool of knowledge, we must recognize that Western society tends to discount the importance of myth and equates technical superiority with superior intelligence. In our modern era, we can only speculate on the human motives and drives of the ancient past that led to these ancestral productions and ensured their preservation for our time. With the recovery of new fragments of these myths of old, however, Western society has begun to appreciate their magnitude and significance, not only to ancient audiences, but also to today's seekers, who now lead widespread efforts to penetrate meanings first expressed in story form more than five thousand years ago.

To equate the ancient with the primitive, as suggested in Budge's use of the derogatory word "spells" for the Pyramid Texts, creates an obstruction in an important pathway toward wisdom. It is important to see for oneself that the ancient understandings are far from primitive. In this book we have focused on creation myths, which we take to include the creation of the heavens and the earth, and of gods and humankind, together with certain necessary details for organizing rulership among the gods and over humankind in the gods' attempts to serve their own needs. Myths that refer to the netherworld or tell mainly about the adventures of human or semidivine heroes, such as Gilgamesh, seem to deal with similar themes from a different perspective. In all we find common allusions to the arising of a greater being that can be equated to higher consciousness.

APPENDIX 2

MEANINGS CONTAINED IN GLYPHS

R. A. Schwaller de Lubicz points out that the images used to write Egyptian hieroglyphs do not compose an alphabet.[1] Much like Hebrew, according to d'Olivet, while glyphs may use illustrations of concrete objects, their combinations in words can evoke a wide range of abstract ideas.[2] A modern reader barely notices when it is necessary to search the context of a word to be sure of its meaning, such as the word *base,* which can mean a foundation, a starting point, or a military installation, along with many additional meanings in science, architecture, and politics. It is not common for a modern reader to ponder the meaning of a letter in a word, but in reaching back to the first written languages in which the myths were recorded, it is important to consider the possible meanings that the letters have, as well as their relationships within the words.

In Egyptian, since the Old Kingdom, words, or collections of glyphs, often require the inclusion of the "determinative" at the ends of most nouns. They guide the reader through the possible meanings, but especially to the cabalistic symbolism of qualities and images that help us choose what the hieroglyphs are intended to convey. That is, the sacred glyphs encompass a breadth of functions and invoke a sense of discrimination in us, rather than maintain a narrow, fixed meaning intended to exclude other meanings, as we find in the alphabetically based words of modern Indo-European languages. In fact, the hieroglyphic system R. A. Schwaller de Lubicz describes seems to be the opposite of our use of the alphabet.

Indo-European languages use words that, in written form, consist of "made-up" letters that are abstract signs. These signs are meaningless images, but in our early education we learn to use them phonetically in combinations that evoke specific concepts or particular objects; we are barely aware of their abstract nature. Gradually, through education, we find other meanings and qualities by using modifying words and additional explanations, enabling us to communicate more exactly, albeit not without some remaining ambiguity. This broadening is required to overcome the restriction of meaning built into the alphabetic foundation of our modern Indo-European languages.

R. A. Schwaller de Lubicz believes that the education of the pharaohs, priests, and other leaders of the society in the use of hieroglyphs directly led to a flourishing of "sacred writing," which invoked the combination of images reflecting complex concepts. He believes that, as explicitly intended, education led to a superior capacity to understand and communicate the traditional, sacred knowledge, one that is available to us today only by specific efforts of study. Proof of this would seem to require that we actually learn the use of a nonalphabetic language, like the one that the Egyptians protected so carefully for thousands of years. Otherwise, we can only admire the possibility offered by his most interesting diagnosis of how to find real meaning, even while admitting that our own comprehension of the language depends on turning the hieroglyphs into their phonetic equivalents and translating them into English.

Even through translation it is possible to detect a remarkable sensitivity in the writings of the ancients. Although we cannot claim to adequately assess all of R. A. Schwaller de Lubicz's theories about ancient Egyptian heiroglyphs, we have been able to recognize the subtlety of meaning in their use. This also seems evident in Sumerian cuneiform and Hebrew lettering. Through comparison of the various versions of the myths, their language of origin, and a detailed look at some of the glyphs, it is evident that the glyphs contain knowledge of complex concepts and their interactions. They contain important pieces of information that can be used to describe esoteric, nonphysical concepts such as higher consciousness.

APPENDIX 3

CREATION REPRESENTED IN NUMBER SYSTEMS

The meaning of *number* has evolved over the millennia. What did they mean to the Ancient Egyptians? Certainly we have evidence that by the time of Pythagoras, circa 500 BCE, Greeks traveled considerably throughout Egypt and the Near East. Certain wise men of Greece gave credit for what they learned to the various active temple centers of Egypt. What has been passed down to us from the Egyptians through the Greeks is known today as the Pythagorean numerology system, and it relates directly to creation and awakening higher consciousness. We draw heavily on the interpretation of the original Egyptian material by R.A. Schwaller de Lubicz and by John Anthony West.[1] In this appendix we address the difference between the quantity represented by a number and the quality that might be represented.

It is remarkable today that these early points of view respecting creation have become so foreign to us in our preoccupation with the theories and concepts promoted in science. Science searches for origins in a purely material context, making it necessary for us to differentiate explicitly between the exoteric and esoteric views before the breadth of what is conveyed in the myths can be fully appreciated. In terms of original creation, the Egyptian god Atum can be seen as the initial differentiation of a "sense of being" out of the void. This is the initiation of "life" in the universe. This is the first "One." Exoterically, it could be equated to the elusive search for the big bang. Esoterically this is the initial awakening of higher consciousness. Such a difference in modes of thinking is made even clearer if we shift our attention from the creation of the "One" out of the void, to the creation of the next number, two. Again, our attention is customarily taken by our habit of counting objects. Our usual mode of thinking says that one must divide into two, resulting simply in the arising of two ones. But this is not the intention in these creation myths, and, indeed, is not allowed in the Pythagorean numerology system; in it, it is patently ridiculous to suppose that there can be two ones. Surely, even for us, there can be only one unity!

According to the Pythagorean system, while we may believe that we can conceive of oneness, or wholeness, this is really only a superficial, intellectual conceit based on our learned behavior in counting. In fact, we experience our world only by perceiving differences between objects and by quantifying their number, rather than by recognizing wholes or absolutes. Thus it is difficult for us to appreciate that we do not divide a one to make a two. In the Pythagorean system, two represents the creation of an essentially new quality, the very essence of which is the quality of division.

Rather than viewing this contradiction—between just counting two items versus recognizing the number two as a step in the creative process—as inconsequential, we should be alert to the fact that in our usual rather inattentive or "automatic" counting mode, we neglect important and significant properties of what numbers can represent. When we look at the process of creation, we cannot simply count things. In the creation myths we are being led to inquire more deeply about the idea that the creation of "one" leads simultaneously to the creation of "two." A reconciliation between the two numbers enables the one and the two together to result in three. The creation of threeness in the Pythagorean numerology system is seen as a new unity. What are the possibilities that this opens to us?

R. A. Schwaller de Lubicz provides us with a remarkable example that illustrates how number concepts can play into ideas about germination and creation.[2] While we shall not repeat his derivation in detail here, we wish to show how he introduces the power of generation by relating it to the mysterious mathematical ratios called ϕ (phi) and π (pi).

The basic idea is that ϕ expresses the division of unity, or the number one, into two parts. This division is, however, not a simple division into two equal parts. Instead, we are led to consider a natural ratio by which division is endlessly repeated in biological systems as either a divisor or multiplier at all scales of space and time, without losing sight of the singular relationship that is invoked by the constant proportion. We can use this ratio to express our perception of the endless power of germination by relating it to the remarkable capacity of the ratio ϕ to divide any linear quantity into two parts in a proportionate division that remains constant despite any changes—divisions or multiplications—in the initial length. That is, there is one unique and simple ratio of two numbers that is not dependent on scale, which when it is expressed in symbols, becomes evident through the act of solving the algebraic equation:

$$a : b :: b : (a+b) \text{ for particular values of "a" and "b"}$$

The precise derivation and solution is given in readily accessible fashion by Lawlor, in explanation of the definition developed in relation to the Egyptian knowledge of this ratio by R. A. Schwaller de Lubicz.[3] The derivation has been known for many years by those interested in sacred geometry and has also been taught to students of art in various universities. As shown by R. A. Schwaller de Lubicz, the value of ϕ is also a simple π such that $\pi = 1.2\ \phi^2$. However, it is not generally known that knowledge of these ratios originated in Egypt or that they are utilized in the proportions of the Great Pyramid. The derivation is, nevertheless, of primary importance to us for better understanding the remarkable insights of this ancient culture, enabling our greater appreciation of its unobtrusive sophistication.

We also observe here that knowledge of the special ratio φ underlies our continued use today of the five-pointed star to signify the starry objects of the sky. Similar illustrations were made over many dynasties on the ceilings of Egyptian tombs. This same ratio establishes the proportions that the Egyptians assigned generally to such "square" spaces as doors, the floor proportions of many of the massive ancient Egyptian temples, and the walls of rooms constructed in those temples. This ratio φ seems to touch some instinctive sense in us that, while widely known to be pleasing, is not often explicitly recognized. Remarkably, it was lost to knowledge after the Egyptian civilization disappeared, until it was apparently "rediscovered" and taught in Pythagorean times in southern Italy. It seems highly probable that knowledge of it was actually transmitted to the early Greek scholars such as Pythagoras during their prolonged visits to the still-remaining Egyptian centers of teaching.

It cannot be emphasized too strongly that if we view myth as leading toward a wisdom that can express a renewed sense of meaning in the modern world, we must be prepared to allow those myths to be interpreted according to different modes of thought. We have already recognized that stories may be viewed as "external," in the sense that they tell of events in a manner that captures our imagination or puts new interpretations on well-known worldly events. But they must also enable us to be led into a world of internal inquiry where perceptions of the "quality" of what is observed enables us to probe them in new ways. While we are less accustomed to the various forms of analogical interpretation, what we do know can at least enable us to see that there is a necessity to open our minds and hearts to unexpected means of perception. The study of the Pythagorean numerology system from this point of view can enable us to appreciate that among modern people there has been an oddity of neglect or partiality, at least in our modes of ordinary thought.

Such limitation, if seen in its true nature as abstraction, has sometimes been loudly decried by philosophers, who maintain that we need to consider how thought must be complemented by "experience," as was insisted on by Goethe.[4] Translation of experience into internal perceptions of both body and emotions leads to new possibilities of comprehension that have been elaborated by Hadot.[5] There is irony in the fact that failure to appreciate the gulf in understanding that has arisen between these two approaches may be largely responsible for the dichotomy that has developed between much of academic Egyptology and the view of Egypt interpreted and presented by R. A. Schwaller de Lubicz. The latter emphasizes that the religious and sometimes intimate and poetic perceptions are of primary importance in the awakening of higher consciousness.

NOTES

Introduction.
The Origin of Our Questions

1. See "Gilgameš, Enkidu and the nether world," http://etcsl.orinst.ox.ac
   .uk/cgi-bin/etcsl.cgi?text=t.1.8.1.4# (accessed January 2015); and Kramer,
   Sumerians.
2. Jung, *Psychology and Religion.*
3. Martin, *Experiment in Depth.*
4. Raffa, *Healing the Sacred Divide.*
5. Barber and Barber, *When They Severed Earth from Sky.*
6. Schwaller de Lubicz, *Symbol and the Symbolic,* 38.
7. Hadot, *Plotinus.*
8. Frye, *Great Code, the Bible and Literature.*
9. Toynbee, *Study of History.*

Chapter One.
Life and Meaning in Myth

1. See "Egyptian Hieroglyphs," http://en.wikipedia.org/wiki/Egyptian_
   hieroglyphs (accessed January 10, 2015).
2. Harpur, *Pagan Christ.*
3. Meyerson, *Linguist and the Emperor.*
4. See "Sir Henry Rawlinson, 1st Baronet," http://en.wikipedia.org/wiki/Sir_
   Henry_Rawlinson,_1st_Baronet (accessed January 10, 2015).

5. de Santillana and von Dechend, *Hamlet's Mill*.

6. Wilkinson, *Rise and Fall of Ancient Egypt*. Offers extensive coverage of the history of ancient Egypt and its interactions with countries in the Near and Middle East.

7. Dalley, *Myths from Mesopotamia*; and Mitchell, *Gilgamesh*.

8. Mitchell, *Gilgamesh*.

Chapter Two.
Myths of Creation and the Awakening of Higher Consciousness

1. Kramer, *Sumerian Mythology*, 130; and Kramer, *Sumerians*.

2. See "Electronic Text Corpus of Sumerian Literature," http://etcsl.orinst .ox.ac.uk/ (accessed January 2015).

3. Kramer, *Sumerian Mythology*.

4. See "Electronic Text Corpus of Sumerian Literature," http://etcsl.orinst .ox.ac.uk/ (accessed January 2015).

5. Heidel, *Babylonian Genesis*.

6. Jacobsen, *Treasures of Darkness*.

7. Dalley, *Myths from Mesopotamia*.

8. Frankfort, *Cylinder Seals*.

9. See "Gilgameš, Enkidu and the nether world," http://etcsl.orinst.ox.ac.uk/ cgi-bin/etcsl.cgi?text=t.1.8.1.4# (accessed January 2015).

10. Heidel, *Babylonian Genesis*.

11. Jacobsen, *Treasures of Darkness*.

12. Dalley, *Myths from Mesopotamia*.

13. Heidel, *Babylonian Genesis*.

14. Dalley, *Myths from Mesopotamia*.

15. Faulkner, *Ancient Egyptian Pyramid Texts*. For example, see Pyramid Text 307, Unis Text 212.

16. Needleman, *What Is God?*

17. Ashby, *Ancient Egyptian Book of the Dead*.

18. Faulkner, *Ancient Egyptian Pyramid Texts*, Pyramid Text 213; Unis Text 146.

19. Dalley, *Myths from Mesopotamia*.

20. Budge, *The Book of the Dead*, 173.

21. Ibid., 28.

22. Rundle Clark, *Myth and Symbol in Ancient Egypt.*

23. Naydler, *Temple of the Cosmos.*

24. Waterfield, *Theology of Arithmetic.*

25. Rundle Clark, *Myth and Symbol in Ancient Egypt,* 42; Pyramid Text 527, lines 1248–49.

26. Ibid., 43; Pyramid Text 600, lines 1652–53.

27. Ibid., 37.

28. Ibid., 45.

29. Frankfort, *Birth of Civilization in the Near East.*

30. Rundle Clark, *Myth and Symbol in Ancient Egypt,* 37.

31. Naydler, *Temple of the Cosmos,* 39.

32. Budge, *Book of the Dead,* cxviii.

33. Rundle Clark, *Myth and Symbol in Ancient Egypt,* 265.

34. Ibid., 58.

35. Ibid., Pyramid Text 301, line 449.

36. Ibid., Pyramid Text 301, line 449.

37. Rundle Clark, *Myth and Symbol in Ancient Egypt,* 59.

38. Ibid., 60; Pyramid Text 506, lines 1099–1100.

39. Naydler, *Temple of the Cosmos,* 54.

40. Frankfort, *Birth of Civilization in the Near East.*

41. Rundle Clark, *Myth and Symbol in Ancient Egypt,* 80.

42. Budge, *Egyptian Religion,* 89.

43. Ibid., 90.

44. Kramer, *Sumerian Mythology,* 39.

45. Budge, *Book of the Dead,* cxviii.

46. See "Thoth," http://wikipedia.org/wiki/Thoth (accessed January 10, 2015).

47. Kramer, *Sumerians,* 174–83.

48. Ibid., 69–70.

49. See "Electronic Text Corpus of Sumerian Literature," http://etcsl.orinst.ox.ac.uk/ (accessed January 2015).

50. Kramer, *Sumerian Mythology,* 70.

51. Ibid., 70.

52. See "Enki and Ninmah: Translation," http://etcsl.orinst.ox.ac.uk/section1/tr112.htm (accessed January 10, 2015).

53. Kramer, *Sumerians,* 66.

54. Ibid., 160–62; and "Gilgameš, Enkidu and the nether world," http://etcsl .orinst.ox.ac.uk/cgi-bin/etcsl.cgi?text=t.1.8.1.4# (accessed January 2015).

55. Kramer, *Sumerians,* 116, Segment F, lines 14–34.

56. See "Me (mythology)," http://Wikipedia.org/wiki/Me_(mythology) (accessed January 10, 2015).

57. Frye, *Great Code, the Bible and Literature.*

58. Heidel, *Babylonian Genesis.*

59. See "Marduk," http://en.wikipedia/org/wiki/Marduk (accessed January 10, 2015).

60. Jacobsen, *Treasures of Darkness.*

61. West, *Serpent in the Sky.*

62. Schwaller de Lubicz, *Temple of Man.*

63. Frankfort, *Birth of Civilization in the Near East.*

Chapter Three.
A Dialogue of the Ages

1. d'Olivet, *Hebraic Tongue Restored.*

2. Ibid., 399.

3. I. Schwaller de Lubicz, *Her-Bak, Egyptian Initiate.*

4. Gunther Plaut, *Torah.*

5. d'Olivet, *Hebraic Tongue Restored.*

Chapter Four.
Gilgamesh: The Struggle for Life

1. Gurdjieff, *Meetings with Remarkable Men.*

2. Jung, *Two Essays in Analytical Psychology,* 71.

3. Sandars, *Epic of Gilgamesh.*

4. Mitchell, *Gilgamesh.*

5. Sandars, *Epic of Gilgamesh,* 62.

6. Ibid., 66.

7. Ibid., 62.

8. Ibid.

9. Kramer, *The Sumerians,* 1489.

10. Sandars, *Epic of Gilgamesh,* 84.

11. Ibid., 97.

12. Ibid., 100.

13. Ibid.

14. Ibid.

15. Ibid., 101.

16. Ibid., 70.

17. Ibid., 102.

18. Ibid.

19. Ibid., 107.

20. Ibid., 112.

21. Ibid., 108.

22. Ibid.

23. Ibid., 113.

24. Ibid.

25. Ibid., 116.

26. Ibid., 117.

27. Ibid.

28. Ibid., 66.

29. Kramer, *Sumerians,* 199–206.

30. Sandars, *Epic of Gilgamesh,* 61.

Chapter Five.
Ancient Egyptian Myths of the Awakening of Higher Consciousness

1. Rundle Clark, *Myth and Symbol in Ancient Egypt.*

2. Schwaller de Lubicz, *Temple of Man.*

3. Ibid., 2.

4. Schwaller de Lubicz, *Symbol and the Symbolic,* 100.

5. Ibid.

6. Budge, *The Book of the Dead,* 32.

7. Schwaller de Lubicz, *Temple of Man.*

8. Sellers, *Death of Gods in Ancient Egypt.*

9. Sandars, *Epic of Gilgamesh,* 88.

10. See "Axial Precession," http://en.wikipedia.org/wiki/Axial_precession (accessed January 10, 2015).

11. See "Ra," http://en.wikipedia.org/wiki/Ra (accessed January 10, 2015).

12. Gardiner, *Egyptian Grammar,* 646.

13. Allen, *The Ancient Egyptian Pyramid Texts,* 73.

14. Schwaller de Lubicz, *Temple of Man,* 359.

Chapter Six.
Journeys through the Netherworld

1. Tracol, *Taste for Things That Are True.*

2. Kingsley, *Reality,* 31.

3. Naydler, *Shamanic Wisdom in the Pyramid Texts.*

4. Eliade, *Shamanism.*

5. Brunton, *Search in Secret Egypt.*

6. Budge, *Book of the Dead.*

7. Dalley, *Myths from Mesopotamia.*

8. Naydler, *Temple of the Cosmos,* 17–25.

9. Ibid., 245.

10. Ibid., 246.

11. Ibid., 247.

12. Kramer, *Sumerian Mythology,* 88–96. Contains the whole of the available text.

13. See "Electronic Text Corpus of Sumerian Literature," http://etcsl.orinst.ox.ac.uk/ (accessed January 2015).

14. Kramer, *Sumerian Mythology,* 91.

15. Ibid.

16. Ibid., 88.

17. Ibid., 89.

18. Ibid., 90.

19. Ibid.

20. Ibid., 91.

21. Ibid., 92.

22. Budge, *Book of the Dead,* 246–47.

23. Ibid., 247.

24. Ibid., 282.

25. See "Arrow of Time," http://en.wikipedia.org/wiki/Arrow_of_time (accessed January 10, 2015).

Chapter Seven.
The Search for Wholeness and Higher Consciousness

1. Budge, *Book of the Dead*. See "Introductory Commentary," ci–cvi, on the Abode of the Blessed, figure 1.

2. Allen, *The Ancient Egyptian Pyramid Texts*.

3. Naydler, *Temple of the Cosmos*.

4. Wilkinson, *Complete Gods and Goddesses of Ancient Egypt*.

5. See "Salem Witch Trials," http://en.wikipedia.org/wiki/Salem_witch_trials#Timeline (accessed January 10, 2015).

6. See "List of Executed for Witchcraft," http://en.wikipedia.org/wiki/List_of_people_executed_for_witchcraft (accessed January 10, 2015).

7. Versluis, *Philosophy of Magic*.

8. Allen, *The Ancient Egyptian Pyramid Texts*, 57.

9. Ibid., 67–68.

10. Ibid., 170.

11. Ibid., 126.

12. Ibid., 128.

13. Ibid., 190.

14. Ibid., 31.

15. Ibid., 39.

16. Ibid.

17. Ibid., 320.

18. Naydler, *Temple of the Cosmos*.

19. Allen, *The Ancient Egyptian Pyramid Texts*, 215.

20. Ibid., 170.

21. Ibid., 171.

22. Naydler, *Temple of the Cosmos*, 125.

23. Kingsley, *Reality*.

24. Ibid., 186.

25. Ibid., 224.

26. Ibid., 29.

27. Versluis, *Philosophy of Magic.*

28. Kingsley, *Reality,* 510–13.

29. Naydler, *Temple of the Cosmos,* 125.

30. Hamilton and Cairns, *Collected Dialogues of Plato.*

Appendix 1.
The Lineage of Myth

1. Budge, *Book of the Dead.*

2. See "Sumer," https://en.wikipedia.org/wiki/Sumer (accessed January 12, 2015).

3. Frankfort, *Cylinder Seals.*

4. Naydler, *Shamanic Wisdom in the Pyramid Texts.*

5. Budge, *Book of the Dead.*

6. Faulkner, *Ancient Egyptian Pyramid Texts*; and Faulkner, *Egyptian Book of the Dead.*

7. Ashby, *Ancient Egyptian Book of the Dead.*

8. Hornung, *Ancient Egyptian Books of the Afterlife.*

9. Naydler, *Shamanic Wisdom in the Pyramid Texts.*

10. Allen, *Middle Egyptian.*

11. Faulkner, *Concise Dictionary of Middle Egyptian.*

12. Naydler, *Shamanic Wisdom in the Pyramid Texts.*

13. Allen, *The Ancient Egyptian Pyramid Texts.*

14. Schwaller de Lubicz, *Temple of Man.*

15. Mitchell, *Gilgamesh,* 5.

16. Johnson, "The Wisdom of Festival," 20–23.

17. Dalley, *Myths from Mesopotamia.*

18. Ibid.

19. Mitchell, *Gilgamesh.*

20. George, *The Babylonian Gilgamesh Epic.*

21. de Santillana and von Dechend, *Hamlet's Mill.*

22. Frankfort, *Birth of Civilization in the Near East,* 56.

23. Kramer, *Sumerians.*

24. See "Sir Henry Rawlinson, 1st Baronet," http://en.wikipedia.org/wiki/Sir_Henry_Rawlinson,_1st_Baronet (accessed January 10, 2015).

Appendix 2.
Meanings Contained in Glyphs

1. Schwaller de Lubicz, *Symbol and the Symbolic.*

2. d'Olivet, *Hebraic Tongue Restored.*

Appendix 3.
Creation Represented in Number Systems

1. West, *Serpent in the Sky.*

2. Schwaller de Lubicz, *Symbol and the Symbolic.*

3. Lawlor, *Sacred Geometry.*

4. Naydler, *Goethe on Science.*

5. Hadot, *Philosophy as a Way of Life.*

BIBLIOGRAPHY

Allen, J. P. *The Ancient Egyptian Pyramid Texts*. Atlanta: Society of Biblical Literature, 2005.

———. *Middle Egyptian: An Introduction to the Language and Culture of Hieroglyphs*. London and New York: Cambridge University Press, 2000.

Ashby, Muata. *The Ancient Egyptian Book of the Dead: The Book of Coming Forth by Day*. Miami: Cruzian Mystic Books, 2000.

Barber, Elizabeth Wayland, and Paul T. Barber. *When They Severed Earth from Sky: How the Human Mind Shapes Myth*. Princeton University Press, 2004.

Brunton, Paul. *A Search in Secret Egypt*. Burdett, New York: Larson, 2007.

Budge, E. A. Wallis. *The Book of the Dead: The Papyrus of Ani*. New York: Dover, 1967.

———. *Egyptian Religion: Egyptian Ideas of the Future Life*. New York: Citadel, 2000.

d'Olivet, Fabre. *The Hebraic Tongue Restored: And the True Meaning of the Hebrew Words Re-Established and Proved by their Radical Analysis*. Translated by N. L. Redfield. New York: Samuel Wiser, 1991.

Dalley, Stephanie. *Myths from Mesopotamia: Creation, the Flood, Gilgamesh, and Others*. Oxford: Oxford University Press, 1989.

de Santillana, G., and H. von Dechend. *Hamlet's Mill*. Boston: David Godine, 1977.

Eliade, Mircea. *Shamanism: Archaic Techniques of Ecstasy*. Princeton, N.J.: Princeton University Press, 1964.

Faulkner, R. O. *The Ancient Egyptian Pyramid Texts*. Oxford: Clarendon Press, 1969.

———. *A Concise Dictionary of Middle Egyptian.* Oxford: Griffith Institute, 1999.

———. *The Egyptian Book of the Dead: The Book of Going Forth by Day.* San Francisco: Chronicle Books, 1972.

Frankfort, Henri. *The Birth of Civilization in the Near East.* New York: Doubleday, 1955.

———. *Cylinder Seals.* London: MacMillan, 1939.

Frye, Northrope. *The Great Code, the Bible and Literature.* Toronto: Academic Press, 1982.

Gardiner, Alan Henderson. *Egyptian Grammar.* 3rd ed. Oxford: Griffith Institute, 1982.

George, A. R. *The Babylonian Gilgamesh Epic: Introduction, Critical Edition and Cuneiform Texts.* Oxford University Press, 2003.

Gunther Plaut, G. *The Torah: A Modern Commentary.* New York: Union of American Hebrew Congregations, 1974.

Gurdjieff, G. I. *Meetings with Remarkable Men.* London: Penguin Group, 1963.

Hadot, Pierre. *Philosophy as a Way of Life: Spiritual Exercises from Socrates to Foucault.* Hoboken, N.J.: Blackwell Publishing, 1995.

———. *Plotinus or The Simplicity of Vision.* Translated by Michel Chase. Chicago and London: University of Chicago Press, 1993.

Hamilton, Edith, and Huntington Cairns, eds. *The Collected Dialogues of Plato.* Bollingen Series 71. Princeton, N.J.: Princeton University Press, 1985.

Harpur, Tom. *The Pagan Christ: Recovering the Lost Light.* Toronto: Tom Allan, 2004.

Heidel, Alexander. *The Babylonian Genesis: The Story of Creation.* 2nd ed. Chicago and London: University of Chicago Press, 1951.

Hornung, Erik. *The Ancient Egyptian Books of the Afterlife.* Ithaca, N.Y.: Cornell University Press, 1999.

Jacobsen, Thorkild. *The Treasures of Darkness.* New Haven and London: Yale University Press, 1976.

Johnson, D. "The Wisdom of Festival." *Parabola: Myth and the Quest for Meaning* 2, no. 2 (1977): 20–23.

Jung, C. G. *Psychology and Religion: West and East.* Vol. 11. New York: Bollingen Foundation, 1958.

———. *Two Essays in Analytical Psychology*. Bollingen Series 20. New York: Pantheon Books, 1953.

Kingsley, Peter. *Reality*. Inverness, Calif.: Golden Sufi Center, 2003.

Kramer, Samuel N. *Sumerian Mythology: A Study of Spiritual and Literary Achievement in the Third Millennium B.C.* Philadelphia: University of Pennsylvania Press, 1972.

———. *The Sumerians: Their History, Culture, and Character*. Chicago and London: University of Chicago Press, 1963.

Lawlor, Robert. *Sacred Geometry: Philosophy and Practice*. London: Thames and Hudson, 1982.

Martin, Percival W. *Experiment in Depth: A Study of the Work of Jung, Eliot and Toynbee*. New York: Pantheon, 1955.

Meyerson, Daniel. *The Linguist and the Emperor: Napoleon and Champollion's Quest to Decipher the Rosetta Stone*. New York: Ballentyne Books (Random House), 2004.

Mitchell, Stephen. *Gilgamesh: A New English Version*. New York: Free Press, 2004.

Naydler, Jeremy. *Goethe on Science: An Anthology of Goethe's Scientific Writings*. Edinburgh: Floris Books, 1999.

———. *Shamanic Wisdom in the Pyramid Texts*. Rochester, Vt.: Inner Traditions, 2005.

———. *Temple of the Cosmos: The Ancient Egyptian Experience of the Sacred*. Rochester, Vt.: Inner Traditions, 1996.

Needleman, Jacob. *What Is God?* New York: Penguin Group, 2009.

Plaut, Gunther. *The Torah: a Modern Commentary, Volume 1 Genesis*. Cincinnati, Ohio: Union of American Hebrew Congregation, 1974.

Raffa, Jean B. *Healing the Sacred Divide: Making Peace with Ourselves, Each Other, and the World*. Burdett, N.Y.: Larson, 2012.

Rundle Clark, Robert T. *Myth and Symbol in Ancient Egypt*. London: Thames and Hudson, 1959.

Sandars, N. K., ed. *The Epic of Gilgamesh: An English Version with an Introduction*. Penguin Classics, 1985.

Schwaller de Lubicz, Isha. *Her-Bak, Egyptian Initiate*. Translated by Ronald Fraser. London: Hodder and Stoughton, 1967.

Schwaller de Lubicz, R. A. *The Egyptian Miracle: An Introduction to the Wisdom of the Temple*. Rochester, Vt.: Inner Traditions, 1985.

————. *Sacred Science: The King of Pharaonic Theocracy.* Translated by André and Goldian VandenBroeck. Rochester, Vt.: Inner Traditions, 1982. Originally published as *Le roi de la théocratie pharaonique,* France, 1962.

————. *Symbol and the Symbolic: Egypt, Science and the Evolution of Consciousness.* Translated by R. Lawlor and D. Lawlor. Brookline, Mass.: Autumn Press, 1957. Reprint, 1978.

————. *The Temple of Man.* Translated by R. Lawlor and D. Lawlor. Rochester, Vt.: Inner Traditions, 1998.

Sellers, Jane B. *The Death of Gods in Ancient Egypt: An Essay on Egyptian Religion and the Frame of Time.* Rev. ed. 1999.

Toynbee, Arnold J. *A Study of History.* An abridgement of volumes 1–6 by D. C. Somerville. New York and London: Oxford University Press, 1947.

Tracol, Henri. *The Taste for Things That Are True.* Rockport, Mass.: Element Books, 1989.

Versluis, Arthur. *The Philosophy of Magic.* Boston, London, and Henley: Arkana Books, 1986.

Waterfield, R., trans. *The Theology of Arithmetic,* attributed to Iamblichus. Grand Rapids, Mich.: Phanes Press, 1988.

West, John A. *Serpent in the Sky: The High Wisdom of Ancient Egypt.* New York: Harper and Row; London: Wildwood House, 1979.

Wilkinson, Richard H. *The Complete Gods and Goddesses of Ancient Egypt.* New York and London: Thames and Hudson, 2003.

Wilkinson, Toby. *The Rise and Fall of Ancient Egypt.* New York: Random House, 2010.

INDEX

Page numbers in *italic* refer to illustrations.

Books of Related Interest

Esoteric Egypt
The Sacred Science of the Land of Khem
by J. S. Gordon

The Path of Initiation
Spiritual Evolution and the Restoration of the
Western Mystery Tradition
by J. S. Gordon

Land of the Fallen Star Gods
The Celestial Origins of Ancient Egypt
by J. S. Gordon

The Temple in Man
by R. A. Schwaller de Lubicz

A Study of Numbers
A Guide to the Constant Creation of the Universe
by R. A. Schwaller de Lubicz

Esoterism and Symbol
by R. A. Schwaller de Lubicz

Sacred Science
The King of Pharaonic Theocracy
by R. A. Schwaller de Lubicz

The Complete Earth Chronicles
by Zecharia Sitchin

INNER TRADITIONS • BEAR & COMPANY
P.O. Box 388
Rochester, VT 05767
1-800-246-8648
www.InnerTraditions.com

Or contact your local bookseller